THE SOCIOLOGY OF THE RESURRECTION

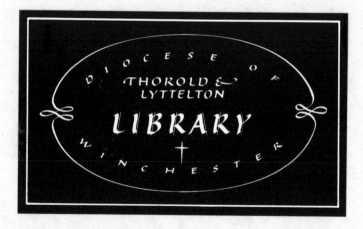

WILLIAM J LUNNY

THE SOCIOLOGY OF THE RESURRECTION

SCM PRESS LTD

Scripture quotations unless otherwise noted are from the
Revised Standard Version of The Bible, Copyright 1946, 1952 and 1971
by the Division of Christian Education of the National Council of Churches, USA.

Cataloguing in Publication data available

334 02335 1

First published in Britain 1989
by SCM Press Ltd
26–30 Tottenham Road, London N1 4BZ
by arrangement with Heron Publishing
Victoria, Canada

Typeset in Canada and
printed in Great Britain by
Billing & Sons Ltd
Worcester

For my Mother

In sure and certain hope

Contents

Preface

This book is intended to be of aid to those who uphold the faith in this secular age. It argues that we can understand the resurrection only if we understand the life and ministry of Jesus. A survey of the resurrection texts and their interpretation by modern theologians precede the main part of the book which is a study of the ministry of Jesus as he taught his disciples to pray, to heal the sick, to exorcize demons and to offer themselves in sacrifice. I have tried to build my interpretation on scripture and to limit the number of footnotes. My indebtedness to others will be apparent.

This work was written while I was on study leave in Australia. May I thank those who have supported us in Victoria, Canada and in Victoria, Australia.

William J. Lunny
Victoria, Canada
November, 1988

Introduction

For many years, while teaching the Christian faith to young people as they prepared for Confirmation, I have spoken of the resurrection of Jesus in terms of the re-formation of a small group or "gang." I have tried to show how Jesus formed this small group of disciples about him, and how he trained them for their role in his mission. I suggested that the meals they had together were very special. Their life together was shattered by the crucifixion. "After three days" the group again found Jesus present with them in the "breaking of bread."[1]

There is little that would be of help to the ordinary pastor in the recent spate of books on the resurrection of Christ.[2] Our young people live in a secular society. They must be enabled to give a reason for the hope that is in them (1 Pet. 3.15). Seeing the re-formation of a group as a part of the resurrection events has many advantages over other ways of attempting to explain what happened. Young people understand how small groups operate. Their social life often consists of the formation and re-formation of "gangs" of friends. Such an explanation helps us to understand what it was that "triggered" the reaction of the disciples. We see that most clearly when the travellers sat down to eat at Emmaus. "He took the bread and blessed, and broke it and gave it to them and their eyes were opened and they recognized him" (Lk. 24.30, 31). When those first disciples gathered to eat together, he appeared in the breaking of bread. In seeing the resurrection this way we are made to understand the connection between the resurrection events and the ministry of Jesus. A study of the resurrection texts alone can fail to make this connection clear. The resurrection was not just one more event in the life of Jesus, it was the culmination and the completion of his incarnate life. It must not be seen in isolation.

If we understand the resurrection to be made manifest by Jesus' participation in a meal with his disciples in those days after the crucifixion, many of the difficulties that are raised by the New Testament reports can be answered. We can understand why "some doubted" (Matt. 28.17), a theme that is found in a number of "appearance" scenes. Even today the experience of Christ's presence is different for different people. In those post-resurrection meals the disciples experienced the power of the Holy Spirit, hence the identification of the risen one with the Holy Spirit that we often find in the writings of St. Paul. They experienced forgiveness, reconciliation, they began to understand the victory that God had won over death. The last supper that Jesus had had with them before the crucifixion began to be more and more important when they came to try to understand the reasons why he had to die. They began to search the scripture so that they could understand their own experience. All of Christian worship, the common meals of the early Christians, the *Agape* or "Love feast," (Jude 1.12) and the eucharist or Lord's Supper may be traced back to these appearances of the risen Lord.

We begin with a study of the reports of the resurrection that we have in the New Testament. It is important that we understand the difficulties that these texts pose for Christian teaching. In Part Two, we will look at some of the more recent attempts to meet the difficulties raised by these texts. Then in the major part of this study we will look for support in scripture for the suggestion that the greater part of the ministry of Jesus was spent in training the twelve. Finally, in Part Four, we will attempt to reconcile the gospel reports with the outline of appearances given by Paul to the Corinthians. We will argue that all the gospel appearances can be seen to be reports, first, of the re-formation of the small group gathered by Jesus as they came to eat together, and then of the beginnings of the growth of that small group into what today we call the Christian Church.

Part One

The Reports of the Resurrection

Near the end of his gospel John tells us that "Jesus did many other signs in the presence of the disciples which are not written in this book; but these are written that you might believe that Jesus is the Christ, the Son of God and that believing you might have life in his name" (Jn. 20.30, 31). What were these "signs" that brought the disciples to belief in the resurrection? How was that relationship that Jesus had built up with his disciples restored?

Paul, who wrote soonest after the events needs only a few sentences to tell the story. His account gives a minimum of information without any indication of place or time, and it differs in many respects from the other gospel versions. Only in Paul's version is there no mention of the women at the tomb. Only in Paul's version are we told that after an appearance to Peter and then to the twelve there is an appearance to "more than five hundred brethren." Then we are told about appearances to James, all the apostles and last of all an appearance to Paul himself (1 Cor. 15.5–9).

When we come to the gospels, the first witnesses to the resurrection are not Peter and the twelve but the women at the empty tomb. In Matthew two women visit the tomb, in Mark three, in Luke at least four and in John, Mary Magdalene alone. She alone is at the tomb in all four gospels. The names of the women in the synoptic gospels vary. Luke and John mention men disciples as being present at the tomb if we accept Luke 24.12 as part of the text. The reasons given for the women coming to the tomb vary. Mark and Luke say that they came to anoint the body of Jesus. Matthew omits this reason and the women come to see a sealed

3

and guarded tomb. John tells us that Joseph of Arimathea and
Nicodemus had already anointed the body before burial. What was
found at the tomb is different in each gospel. In Mark the women enter
the tomb and find a young man in a white robe. In Matthew as the
women arrive at the tomb an angel descends from heaven and rolls away
the stone. The guards fall in a faint. The angel gives his message outside
the tomb telling the women "to come and see the place where he lay"
(Matt. 28.6). In Luke, when they enter the tomb the women are sur-
prised by two men in dazzling apparel. John has Mary find the stone removed when she comes to the tomb and her reaction is to run and tell
Peter. Later she stoops to look into the tomb and she sees two angels in
white.

An even more confused matter is the appearances of the risen Christ.
Each gospel writer gives a different answer to questions about the number, the form, the where and the when of the appearances. Mark ends
his gospel with the words "for they were afraid" (Mk. 16.8). He does
not record a resurrection appearance. A later hand has added appearances to Mary Magdalene at the tomb, to two other disciples as they
walked in the country and then to the eleven all together. There is an appearance to the women at the tomb in Matthew, and to Mary Magdalene
alone in John. Matthew has one appearance to the eleven, whereas Luke
had an appearance at Emmaus as well as an appearance to the gathered
disciples and he refers to an appearance to Peter alone. He also adds
other appearances in the book of Acts. John has two appearances to the
disciples and in an epilogue, Chapter 21, he describes a further meeting.
Many of these reports are so different that it is very difficult to see
where they overlap. We cannot tell how many appearances are recorded. Another difficulty is to tell where these appearances took place.
They occurred in Galilee, according to John 21 and Matthew. This is
also the setting implied in the original ending to Mark. The appearances
occurred in Jerusalem and its vicinity according to Luke and John 20.
There are other problems. Luke has the risen Christ moving toward an
ascension that would end his visible presence. In Matthew's account
however, Christ, already ascended and exalted, tells his disciples that
he will be "with them to the end of the age" (Matt. 28.16–20). In John
the risen Christ confers the Spirit, whereas in Luke he promises the
Spirit that will be given after his departure. In John the risen Christ tells
Mary Magdalene not to touch him because he has not yet ascended,
while in Luke's account of the Thomas story, Jesus invites the disciples
to touch him.

It seems that Paul and each of the gospel writers has his own distinctive understanding of the nature of resurrection. The discrepancies in the accounts come as a result of these different understandings of the event. Let us look at their reports in turn.

1. 1 Corinthians 15.3–8

The earliest account of the Easter events that we have is the listing of the appearances made by Jesus in a letter written to the Corinthian Church about 50 A.D. Paul says to the Corinthians, "For I delivered to you as of first importance what I also received, that Christ died for our sins in accordance with the scriptures, that he was buried, that he was raised on the third day in accordance with the scriptures and that he appeared to Cephas, then to the twelve. Then he appeared to more than five hundred brethren at one time, most of whom are still alive, though some have fallen asleep. Then he appeared to James, then to all the apostles. Last of all, as to one untimely born, he appeared also to me" (1 Cor. 15.3–8). Paul is dealing with a very special situation in this epistle. He has heard that there are people at Corinth that deny the possibility of resurrection. The Christian life for these Corinthians must have been a kind of gnostic life that emphasized this world. Paul seems to think that this is what has been taught by others who have denied that Paul has the right to be called an apostle (1 Cor. 9.1, 2). Paul replies to these false teachers with a series of arguments. If there is no resurrection, why do you baptize for the dead? (1 Cor. 15.29). If there is no resurrection those who have died have perished (1 Cor. 15.18). If Christ is raised from the dead there must be resurrection (1 Cor. 15.13).

The main argument is that he has taught what has been taught by others, the "them" he refers to in 1 Corinthians 15.10 are presumably some at least of those listed as witnesses of the resurrection. As an "eyewitness" himself, Paul had "delivered" to the Corinthians what he had "received." Both these words are technical words for the handing down of tradition. The teaching that had founded the Corinthian Church was the teaching that was taught by all who had been chosen for an appearance of Christ. Not only was his teaching the same as those listed, "Am I not an apostle? Have I not seen the Lord?" (1 Cor. 9.1), but Paul was also making the point that his teaching had the same authority as those in his list. In this way he continues the condemnation of those who would form parties at Corinth (1 Cor. 1.11f, 3.4f).

The first part of our passage (1 Cor. 3–5) could have been "delivered" to Paul any time after his conversion but most probably he would have been given the basic formula as part of his initial instruction as a Christian. If, as it seems, he was converted shortly after the resurrection preaching began, (Acts gives the impression that it took place very early), the testimony of 1 Corinthians 15.3–8 goes back almost to the events described.[3] The note about some of the five hundred having "fallen asleep" and his mention of himself as a witness means that at least part of this passage is his own composition. These first four clauses seem to be part of the original formula. They are all introduced by the word "that" and read like a creedal formula. The language then changes and "he appeared" is repeated without an introductory "that."

Why then did Paul add other names to what may have been the traditional formula? He wanted to attack the suggestion that there was rivalry in the Church. He may also have wanted to narrow the time between his own conversion and the "third day" and yet provide the widest possible basis for the witness to the resurrection. We must remember that he is going on to argue "Whether then it was I or they, so we preach and so you believed" (1 Cor. 15.11). Paul would seem to be grounding the authority of those who were the leaders of the Church on their experience of a resurrection appearance.

It is interesting that when Paul speaks of his first visit to Jerusalem after his conversion he makes a point of saying that he did not see any of the apostles except Peter and James, the brother of the Lord (Gal. 1.18, 19). If he received from them both their own resurrection experiences and those of their own groups we can account for the clear parallelism found in the list that Paul has put before us without having to suggest that the Corinthians knew of two lists comprising an appearance to an individual, his group and followers. Paul wanted to teach the Corinthians that the Christian Church was one single, whole organization. To do this he combined these two traditions. He uses the adverb "then" to make it clear that these appearances occurred in chronological order.

The appearance to Cephas and the twelve is exactly the way the reestablishment of a small group would be described after that group had been shattered by the loss of its leader. Peter, throughout the gospels was always a member of the inner circle of disciples within the group. If the group re-formed it would have to have been about a new leader. The use of the word Cephas supports this suggestion. Simon Bar-jona received this name (Aramaic *Kepha*, Greek *Petros*: Rock) because he was to be the foundation stone of the new community (Matt. 16.17–19). So the appearance to the twelve confirms the promise to them that they would "sit on twelve thrones judging the twelve tribes of Israel" (Matt. 19.28). The appearances to Peter and the twelve have a common function. In them Jesus founds the eschatological community, the Christian Church.

If the appearance to Peter was completely separate from the appearance to the twelve, it is difficult to understand why the record of such an appearance had disappeared by the time the gospels came to be written. Luke mentions the tradition of an appearance to Peter in the Emmaus story in which the two disciples, on their return to Jerusalem and before they can tell their own story, are told "The Lord has risen indeed, and has appeared to Simon" (Lk. 24.34). Matthew, with his special interest in Peter, does not mention an appearance to Peter and even drops the mention of Peter in his version of Mark 16.7. It is possible that Jesus appeared to Peter and the others of the group on the same occasion. What Paul is saying is that Peter was the first of the twelve to notice the presence of Jesus. This would explain why a single "he appeared" functions for both. Jesus appeared to Peter and "then" moments later the others saw him.

The appearance to the "more than five hundred brethren at one time" is also given without detail. Nowhere else in the New Testament are we told of an appearance to such a large group. The only large gathering reported is the glossolalia incident reported in Acts where "there were added that day three thousand souls and they devoted themselves to the apostles' teaching and fellowship, to the breaking of bread and the prayers" (Acts 2.41, 42). Perhaps this report in Acts can help us understand Paul's report. The appearances to Peter and the the twelve effect the foundation of the Christian community. The appearance to the "more than five hundred brethren" tells us of that community coming into operation. The word "brethren" is often used by Paul to describe Christian believers. At one or more of those gatherings of the early Church for "the breaking of bread and prayers," Jesus appeared in their midst. As the relationship that Jesus had built with his disciples was reestablished by his appearance to Peter and the twelve, so his relationship with the "crowds that followed" was reestablished by his appearance to the five hundred brethren.

What may perhaps be a rival list placed next by Paul begins with James and we must assume that he is speaking of James, the brother of the Lord. He was not a disciple of Jesus in his earthly ministry (Mk.

3.21f, Jn. 7.5) but he is soon found playing an important role in the life
of the early Church (Gal. 2.1–10, Acts 15.13, 21.18). In Acts 1.12f,
Peter is listed with the others of the twelve and then we are told they
"with one accord devoted themselves to prayer, together with the
women and Mary the mother of Jesus and with his brothers." As the appearance to Peter meant his restoration after his denial of Jesus (cf., Lk.
22.32, Jn. 21.15–17) and the reestablishment under his leadership of
the small group formed by Jesus, so the appearance of Jesus to James
resulted in his conversion and the establishment under his leadership of
the group that Paul calls "all the apostles." On Paul's second visit to
Jerusalem, to attend the so-called "apostolic conference" (Gal.
2.1–10), James is mentioned first as though he was in charge of the
apostolic mission. Again, it is James who sends "certain men" to
Antioch (Gal. 2.12). We get a similar impression when we read Acts,
for here also he plays a leading role at the conference (Acts 15.13) with
Paul reporting to him about his mission policies (Acts 21.18).

When we come to study "all the apostles," we should note that as
Peter may be included among the twelve with that appearance of Jesus,
so James may be included with the appearance of Jesus to "all the
apostles." This brings us to the vexed problem of the identification of
"all the apostles." In distinction from the evangelists and particularly
from Luke, when Paul speaks of them in 1 Corinthians 15.7 or in
Galatians 1.17–19 he seems to refer to a cohesive group living in or
near Jerusalem that was in existence before Paul's conversion. Their
claim to apostleship appears to be based on a resurrection appearance.
The use of the masculine form of the noun does not preclude the possibility that women were members of this circle in Jerusalem. The word
could well be used in the generic sense. The summary in Acts 1.14
reflects a tradition in which women were part of the nucleus of this
group. Paul also seems to speak of other apostles who do not base their
claim to the office on being witnesses of the resurrection as much as on
their missionary work. They travelled from city to city relying on
people's support (1 Cor. 9.1f). Some appear to have travelled with their
wives (1 Cor. 9.5). Some seem to have had nasty things to say about
Paul (2 Cor. 10.10–13). Paul calls himself and his fellow missionaries
"apostles." We know some of their names, Barnabas, (Acts 14.4f),
Timothy and Silvanus (1 Thess. 2.6f) and Andronicus and Junias (a fe-
male name) (Rom. 16.7). As Paul emphasized, in his dispute with the
Jerusalem apostles, that he too had seen the Lord, so he insists in his
argument with the other apostles that he can claim for himself all the

signs and visions that they are so proud of experiencing (1 Cor. 2.4, Rom. 15.19, 2 Cor. 12.1–7). For Paul, apostleship is proved by the fruits of missionary work (1 Cor. 9.15–18). The decisive mark of an apostle is the acceptance of the labors and the sufferings connected with mission (1 Cor. 4.8–13, 2 Cor. 11, 12).

The appearance to Paul has its own problems. When he lists his own appearance experience he gives no hint that he thought his experience was any different from that of the others. He makes the point in 1 Corinthians 9.1 that he saw Jesus. Yet when we read Luke's account an appearance to Paul is ruled out because of the Ascension. The three accounts in Acts (9.1–22, 22.3–21, 26.1–23) are "visions." Paul never elaborates on what he means by "seeing" the Lord and therefore we cannot tell whether the accounts in Acts, rather inconsistent in themselves, can give us any certain knowledge of Paul's experience.

We will return to Paul's account of the resurrection appearances when we have considered the gospel accounts. We will then attempt to locate them geographically and understand their purpose.

2. Mark

Mark is the only gospel writer not to give us an account of the resurrection appearances. The scholarly consensus is that Mark's original text ended with the words "for they were afraid" (Mk. 16.8). All that follows is a later addition not found in the more important manuscripts. Some have suggested that the original ending was lost or destroyed. Many have found it difficult to believe that a gospel would end, as it does in Greek (Mk. 16.8) with the preposition "for." The other endings do read as though they were written by other hands. There are many other difficulties with this account of the empty tomb.

Within a few verses, Mark gives us three lists of the women involved in his story and these lists are inconsistent. It is also difficult to accept the reason given by Mark for the visit of the women to the tomb. He tells us it was so "they might go and anoint him" (Mk. 16.1). The completion of burial rites on a Sunday morning after the body was buried on Friday, considering the climate, is unbelievable. From what we know of the burial rites of the time it is likely that Joseph of Arimathea would have done everything that was required. It is difficult to understand why a Jew of such important standing would not fulfill a duty he volunteered to perform, apparently out of religious conviction. In a missionary

speech attributed to Paul in Acts 13.29 we are told that the burial was
carried out by those who "asked Pilate to have him killed" (Act 13.28).
Those "religious men," in using a tomb would have followed all the
Jewish laws and customs. The other gospel writers are uncomfortable
with the reason given by Mark for the visit of the women to the tomb.
Matthew has the women go "to see the sepulchre" (Matt. 28.1). Luke
transfers the preparation of the spices and ointments to the day of the
crucifixion. He must have felt that there was little time for such preparation on the third day and perhaps he did not know that such work as the
burial of the dead was allowed on the Sabbath. John has Mary Magdalene simply go to the tomb that morning "early, while it was still
dark" (Jn. 20.1). The other evangelists also omit Mark's passage that
tells us that the women wondered, as they walked toward the site, who
they would get to roll away the great stone that served as a door to the
tomb. Mark would have us believe that the women set out prepared to
anoint the body and yet they were not prepared to get access to the
body. Matthew has an angel come as they arrive and he rolls back the
stone. In the other gospel accounts the tomb is found open.

A period of mourning was prescribed after all funerals. In the Old
Testament we are told that it lasted seven days (Gen. 50.10, 1 Sam.
31.13, 1 Chr. 10.12, Sirach 22.12). It was customary for friends and relations to visit the tomb of a loved one, especially until the third day, the
day the soul was thought to part finally from the body. There is no need
to suggest any special reason other than the natural desire to visit the
place of burial. Our difficulty is in understanding why Mark gives the
reason that he does for the visit of the women, not the visit itself.

In Mark, the women enter the tomb and find "a young man sitting on
the right side, dressed in a white robe" (Mk. 16.5). They react with fear
and shock. He tells them that Jesus is risen and they are to "tell his disciples and Peter that he is going before you into Galilee" (Mk. 16.7).
We can take this to mean that they are to tell the disciples and especially
Peter that Jesus has gone to Galilee and will await them there or we can,
more naturally, take it to mean that Jesus will lead them to Galilee, as a
shepherd leads his sheep (Mk. 14.28). The reaction of the women after
this instruction was to flee the tomb "for trembling and astonishment
had come upon them and they said nothing to any one" (Mk. 16.8).

The familiar ending to Mark's gospel that appears in the King James
version has been considered to be a later non-Markan addition by almost
all of today's scholars. It is often thought that this longer "canonical"
ending is a summary of the appearances recorded at the end of the other

gospels. Yet there are real differences from what could be called the parallel accounts. The use of the active "when he rose" (Mk. 16.9) is different from the form used in the other gospels. There, Jesus is usually seen as the object of God's action. Mary Magdalene tells the others of her encounter as they "mourned and wept" (Mk. 16.10). These words are used throughout scripture to describe the normal behavior at a funeral but they are not used by the other evangelists. The appearance to the eleven is made "as they sat at table" (Mk. 16.14). In the Emmaus story where an appearance at table is mentioned, it is an appearance to two disciples. Only in this passage does Jesus reproach the eleven for their unbelief (Mk. 16.14). The commission of the disciples is independent of those in the other gospels. The statement about the Ascension differs from those of Luke. We may conclude that this passage is an independent tradition that has been handed down to us by being attached to Mark's gospel at some early time.

3. Matthew

If we assume that Matthew had Mark's gospel with the short ending when he came to write his version of the resurrection events, we can see the influence of the Church tradition he represented by the way he completed his account. The greater part of the material added by Matthew concerns the story of the guard at the tomb. On the very day they are commanded to rest, the Sabbath, the enemies of Jesus are hard at work in a vain attempt to place a seal on their action of putting Jesus to death. To understand how this tale came to be told we must realize that, to the Jewish mind, resurrection meant resurrection from the grave. When Christians told of Jesus being raised on the third day, the Jews replied, "show us the tomb." When they were shown the tomb, they suggested that the body had been removed by the disciples. Matthew's story is thus told in reaction to Jewish polemic. The repeated mention of the "third day" in this passage shows that in the early Church the "third day" was identified with the discovery of the empty tomb. It can be thought that the Christian preaching of the resurrection on the "third day" gave rise to the "empty tomb" tradition. It would seem more likely that the discovery of the empty tomb on the third day gave rise to the preaching of the resurrection on the "third day."

When we come to study the visit of the women to the tomb, we find that Mark is followed, with minor changes designed to remove discrepancies. The rock is rolled away by an angel. Only two women come to the tomb, the same two that were at the burial. There are various other changes, the most important is the removal of the statement that the women told no one "for they were afraid" (Mk. 16.8). The angel sends them to tell the disciples, no mention of Peter, that "he is risen from the dead" (Matt. 28.7). They depart with "fear and great joy" (Matt. 28.8).

We are told that the women ran to report to the disciples but as they left the area they are confronted by Jesus. They worship him and attempt to take hold of him. Jesus repeats the message of the angel. This appearance to the women at the tomb is not recorded by Mark or Luke, but John 20.11–18 records an appearance to Mary Magdalene at this point. When we remember the prejudice against women as witnesses found in Judaism at this time, and that Paul's purpose when writing 1 Corinthians 15.5f was to place himself in a list of male leaders of the Church who were also witnesses, and that Mark's short ending does not tell of any encounters with the risen Jesus, it seems probable that Matthew has here recorded an important tradition. He perhaps knew only that Jesus appeared to the women. He did not know what took place or what was said. This would explain why he has Jesus repeat what the angel has already told the women.

Matthew concludes his gospel with an appearance to the eleven on a Galilean mountain. The resurrection element in the passage is passed over very briefly: "when they saw him they worshipped him; but some doubted" (Matt. 28.17). Matthew is more concerned with the commission of the disciples. It is probably a Matthaean composition as it has a very high proportion of words that belong to his special vocabulary. It reads like a royal decree, such as those that we find in the Old Testament (Gen. 45.9–11, 2 Chron. 36.23). The eleven are now to go and "make disciples of all nations" (Matt. 28.19). In his gospel Matthew had emphasized that both Jesus and the disciples had confined their mission to Israel (Matt. 10.5f, 15.24). "All nations" can be understood to mean that now the mission is confined to the gentiles but probably it means all people. The eleven are like scribes who have "been trained for the kingdom of heaven" (Matt. 13.52). They are now to go and make disciples, baptize and teach. As Jesus has taught them all things they are now commissioned to teach and interpret what Jesus has taught them.

In light of the emphasis on the disciples teaching "all nations," we can better understand the rather puzzling reference to "the mountain to which Jesus had directed them" (Matt. 28.16). Matthew attaches great theological significance to "the mountain" as a place of revelation. It is the place of the transfiguration (Matt. 17.1–14). This is where the disciples have been taught what they must now teach. The great "Sermon on the Mount" (Matt. 5.1f), delivered to the disciples at this place, must now be delivered by those same disciples "to all nations." Their task is "teaching them to observe all that I have commanded you" (Matt. 28.20). This same place may also be associated with the feeding of the five thousand. Directly after the miraculous feeding, Jesus, "after he had dismissed the crowds, (he) went up into the hills (mountains) by himself to pray" (Matt. 14.23).

4. Luke

Luke, in writing his gospel, used his material in a particular way. We can see that he continued the pattern he had established when he came to record the discovery of the empty tomb. He followed the events in Mark, correcting what he saw as mistakes or difficulties and working in his own special material as he went along. For instance, he explains why the anointing was delayed (Lk. 23.56): the Sabbath rest interfered. Most of the changes that Luke makes from Mark, in the names of the women, in the reason for their visit, the question about opening the tomb, can be explained in this way. The other changes he has made allow him to tell the stories from his own special material of the appearances in and about Jerusalem. The reference to Galilee is made into a remembrance of Galilee (Lk. 24.6); the angel recalls how Jesus had told them what would happen "while he was still in Galilee." When the women remember this Galilean prophecy of Jesus, of their own volition they return "to the eleven and to all the rest" (Lk. 24.9).

In Luke's gospel, Galilee is in the past. Jerusalem is the center from which the gospel is to be carried to all the world and particularly to Rome. Jerusalem, therefore, becomes the scene of the resurrection appearances. It would seem that the focus on Jerusalem in the gospel and the final focus on Rome in the Acts of the Apostles is part of Luke's overall scheme. This would explain why he has suppressed Mark's reference to Jesus "going before" the disciples to Galilee and the promise about Galilee in the prediction of the passion in Mark 14.28.

The first of Luke's special material obviously bears some relationship to the story in John's gospel that tells of Peter's dash to the tomb. Yet there are real differences between the two accounts. The passage is omitted in most "Western" texts and this adds to the confusion. Luke and John seem to share a common tradition that tells of certain disciples being nearby when the women found the empty tomb. The most prominent among those disciples was Peter. Luke repeats this tradition in verse 24 of the Emmaus story (Lk. 24.13f).

The Emmaus story is without parallel in the other gospels. It is by far the most carefully constructed resurrection story and it is certainly the longest. A stranger joins two disciples as they walk to Emmaus. As they near the village the disciples beseech him, as in prayer, to abide with them. The actions of Jesus at table are described in many of the same words that are used at other meals in the gospels, at the feeding of the five thousand, at the last supper. When the disciples understand the truth of the scripture as interpreted to them by the stranger, Jesus takes the bread, blesses it, breaks it and gives it to them "and their eyes were opened and they recognized him" (Lk. 24.31). The story ends with the disciples returning to Jerusalem where they find that Jesus has appeared to Peter.

Luke repeats all the features of the Emmaus passage in the next scene in his gospel. There is teaching about death and resurrection foretold in scripture. There is a meal scene in which Jesus takes a piece of fish and eats it before the disciples. There are similarities between this passage and the report in John 20.19–29. In both, the location is Jerusalem, the time is Easter evening, both use the phrase "stepped into their midst" and in both there is a display and an invitation to touch the body of Jesus. Both passages connect the appearance with the mission of the Church and the gift of the Spirit. Both appearances take place at a meal.

It is in Luke that we have the clearest connection between a meal of joy and thanksgiving and the appearance of Jesus to the disciples. At Emmaus "when he was at table with them" he broke bread and "their eyes were opened and they recognized him" (Lk. 24.31). That evening in Jerusalem they gave him a piece of fish and he "ate before them" (Lk. 24.43). In Acts 1.4 the word that is often translated "staying" may also be translated "eating." It seems very probable, when we consider the other passages in Luke, that the passage should read "appearing to them during forty days and speaking of the kingdom of God and while eating with them he charged them not to depart from Jerusalem" (Acts 1.3, 4). In Acts 10.41, Peter's sermon includes the passage "not to all the people, but to those who were chosen by God as witnesses, who ate and drank with him after he rose from the dead." In an attempt to demonstrate the physical reality of the resurrection some of these passages may have been developed in an apologetic direction. However, the meal motif plays a very important part in Luke's reports of the resurrection appearances.

5. John

John's gospel has two chapters that tell of the resurrection. The one, Chapter 20, reports on the tradition connected with Jerusalem. The other, Chapter 21, perhaps added by another hand, draws on the tradition connected with a Galilean appearance.

John has structured the events in Jerusalem so that Mary's encounter with Jesus does not overshadow the discovery of the empty tomb by Peter with John. Indeed, the priority of Peter and the early faith of John and the relationship between the two of them seem to be the reasons behind this story. John may have put together separate traditions at this point. The way Mary reports to the disciples "They have taken the Lord out of the tomb and we do not know where they have laid him" (Jn. 20.2), using the first person plural pronoun, is perhaps a trace of an earlier story in which more than one woman was present. When Peter and John have gone, Mary is again present at the tomb and Jesus appears. The Beloved Disciple saw (the empty tomb) and believed. Mary does not recognize Jesus when he speaks to her. This scene is like other resurrection appearances that emphasize that these encounters are not ordinary physical appearances but revelatory encounters (Gal. 1.16, Lk. 24.31, Matt. 28.17). The message Jesus gives Mary is to be taken to "my brethren." She reports to the disciples.

Angels are prominent in all the resurrection reports of the empty tomb, including John's. Perhaps he saw the angel's presence as a fulfillment of the promise made at the beginning of the gospel "you shall see greater things than these... you will see heaven opened and the angels of God ascending and descending upon the Son of Man" (Jn. 1.50, 51). This is the meaning of the message Mary is to convey to the disciples: "Say to them, I am ascending to my Father and your Father, to my God and your God" (Jn. 20.17). This is why Mary is told "Do not hold me."

There follows an appearance to the disciples that no doubt is meant to invoke a picture of the group gathered for meditation at supper, "on the first day of the week." The doors are shut in face of persecution, perhaps a familiar situation by the time John came to write his gospel. Again, a week later, on another Lord's Day, the group is again gathered at supper time. In this setting Thomas is invited to touch Jesus and his response is "My Lord and my God" (Jn. 20.28).

In Chapter 21, Jesus appears to seven disciples by the sea of Galilee. Taken by itself, it gives the impression of a single appearance, unconnected with any other. One could think that it was the first and only appearance of Jesus to the disciples. In the Johannine style the apostolic mission is dramatized by the story of the great catch of fish. A meal is prepared and served by Jesus himself. The story seems to have some relationship to the story in Luke 5.1–10 of the disciples fishing after they have toiled all night.

6. Conclusion

This study of the resurrection tradition has not been very detailed. We have simply pointed to the material that will be used in our final section as we try to understand the resurrection. We can see that any attempt to harmonize these reports will be difficult. They differ from one another more in the telling of the Easter events than in the telling of any other part of the common story. What we have are very separate expressions of Easter faith. Each was written by an evangelist to serve as the ending and completion of his gospel story. It is unlikely that any of the evangelists ever imagined that their account would one day be placed side by side with other accounts of the Easter events.

It is difficult to reconcile the geographical difference. It is even more difficult to reconcile the more profound differences such as that between a risen Jesus who appears very like a resuscitated body immediately recognizable, and other accounts of a Christ who is not recognized unless through some word or action.

Our task is to understand how a small group of men, gathered and trained by Jesus, came together again in the presence of Jesus after the crucifixion and began to proclaim that God had raised Jesus from the dead.

Part Two

Resurrection Studies

A.M. Ramsey, in his book, *The Resurrection of Christ,* makes the point that for the first disciples "the Gospel without the Resurrection was not merely a Gospel without its final chapter: it was not a Gospel at all."[4] The disciples had been attracted to Jesus by his moral teaching, and the integrity of his character, but he had led them into perplexity, paradox and darkness. They would have remained in that condition had Jesus not been raised from the dead. As Paul put it "If Christ has not been raised, then our preaching is in vain and your faith is in vain" (1 Cor. 15.14). Evangelism and faith are impossible and empty without the resurrection. Ramsey goes on to point out that all Christian preaching is dependent on the resurrection. It was the resurrection that showed that Jesus was the Christ, who through that divine victory over death and sin was the means of the coming of the kingdom of God. Early Christian preaching taught that the resurrection was "according to the scriptures," therefore we have an abundance of proof texts such as those from the fifty-third chapter of Isaiah or the Psalms. In this preaching the resurrection was likened to a new act of creation and to a new Exodus.[5]

The resurrection was the cause of what Ramsey calls a stupendous change: "Hebrew monotheists, without forsaking their monotheism, worshipped Jesus as Lord."[6] Christian worship grew about this event, and about the Lord's Supper on the Lord's Day.

The resurrection was also the source of Christian belief. The God that Christians came to worship was the God that "raised from the dead Jesus our Lord" (Rom. 4.24). In 1 Peter (1.21) we have, "Through him you have confidence in God, who raised him from the dead and gave him glory, so that your faith and hope are in God." As Ramsey puts it, "Christian theism is Resurrection theism."[7] Ramsey also makes the point that Christian ethics are resurrection ethics. Ethics are defined and made possible by those who are "raised with Christ" and are therefore able to "seek the things that are above" (Col. 3.1). Indeed "It is Christ Jesus who died, yes, who was raised from the dead, who is at the right hand of God, who intercedes for us" (Rom. 8.34).

How do we understand these reports of the resurrection that we have surveyed? How do we explain this event that came to be the basis of all Christian preaching, Christian worship and Christian belief? Those who have studied the texts have answered this question in various ways.

The traditional interpretation sees the resurrection as an event in the life of Jesus. It is not that the accounts of the women at the empty tomb and the various accounts of the appearances verify the faith. These events are seen as completing the work of God in Jesus, the Christ. The resurrection is an event in the destiny of Jesus. As Karl Barth put it, "For unless Christ's resurrection was a resurrection of the body, we have no guarantee that it was the decisively acting Subject Jesus Himself who rose from the dead."[8]

Then there are those who place their emphasis on the followers of Jesus and see the resurrection as an event in their lives. In this way these writers are able to avoid any suggestion of the miraculous, any emphasis on the importance of history and the reliability of the New Testament reports of the resurrection. Bultmann, for instance, sees the reality of the resurrection being brought into being by the growth of faith in what Jesus did on the cross. As he puts it, "This is because the redemptive significance of the cross (and therefore the resurrection also) can only become apparent to those who submit to being crucified with Christ, who accept him as Lord in their daily lives."[9] The resurrection is not to be thought of as an event in the life of Jesus, "If the event of Easter Day is in any sense an historical event additional to the event of the cross, it is nothing else than the rise of faith in the risen Lord."[10] Jesus lives on in the proclamation of the Church, in this way he still summons us to a decision of faith.

Between these two positions there are some scholars who concentrate their study on the reports of the resurrection and then look back from those reports to explain and understand the ministry of Jesus. Reginald Fuller, in his book *The Formation of the Resurrection Narratives,* provides an example of this method. After a thorough examination of the

New Testament narratives, Fuller tells us that:"the proper thing to do is to interpret the story (the empty tomb pericope), like the appearance stories, in accordance with the Evangelists' intention. That... intention of the Evangelists is to assert not the resuscitation of Jesus' body, but his translation into eschatological existence."[11] He then explains that the disciples did not "see" this happen. An event like that belongs to the transcendent eschatological future. This event, only expressed by myth or analogy, was revealed to them by God. The purpose then of the resurrection narratives was to give that faith expression.[12] They are not literal descriptions of what took place. Because of this experience of God, the disciples were enabled to understand the whole ministry of Jesus. As Fuller puts it, "The whole structure of Christian faith (The Christ event, *kerygma,* sacrament, church) depends on the presence of the eschatological in, with and under temporal events."[13]

There is another group of scholars who approach the subject in another way. They tend to look forward, from the life and ministry of Jesus, to explain and interpret the resurrection. An example of this position is provided by the book *Jesus* by Edward Schillebeeckx.[14] He attempts to show that because of the disciples' involvement with Jesus in his ministry they came to a faith in the continuing activity of Jesus after the crucifixion. In their time with Jesus the disciples gradually came to believe that Jesus was the prophet sent from God, that he was in a way, a new Moses. After the crucifixion the disciples scattered and escaped violence. Some of them, led by Peter, studied the scriptures about the promised one. The reports of the empty tomb and the appearances of Jesus are their attempts to explain what they had experienced. They tell of a series of resurrection visions that disclosed the continuing activity of Jesus. The disciples' "renewed fellowship" with Jesus confirmed the religious experience that came from their study of scripture. Their experience of grace and forgiveness meant that living communication with Jesus continued after his death.

There are, therefore, four ways of understanding the resurrection in recent theology. There are those who attempt to portray the resurrection reports as eyewitness accounts of what took place. At the opposite extreme there are those who would reduce these accounts to legend and mythology. Between these two positions there are those who work from the accounts themselves to look back on the ministry of Jesus to reach an understanding of what is meant and those who work from the ministry of Jesus to look forward to reach an understanding of the resurrection. We shall examine one recent example of each of these positions.

1. M. J. Harris

The traditional position, which sees the resurrection as an event in the earthly life of Jesus, was put forward by Bishop B.F. Westcott in two books written at the end of the nineteenth century, *The Gospel of the Resurrection* (1866) and *The Revelation of the Risen Lord* (1881).[15] In his first book, Westcott was very certain that those who would deny what the scripture taught on the resurrection could only do so if they had arrived at the accounts with the assumption that such an event was impossible. In his second book he emphasizes that the resurrection is a "new revelation" and therefore it is different from other historical events. It follows therefore that it is impossible to prove these events historically.

No such hesitation about the historical facts occurs in *Raised Immortal* by M.J. Harris (1983).[16] He sets out to "examine not only the New Testament data on resurrection and on immortality as separate themes, but also, and more importantly, the relation between these two ideas in New Testament teaching."[17] His study of the "data" is very conservative.

Harris begins by looking at the three major passages in the synoptics in which Jesus speaks of his coming death and resurrection (Mk. 8.31–33, 9.30–32, 10.32–34, par.). In Mark's gospel these passages are placed at important points in the narrative. After each prediction there is some misunderstanding by the disciples to which Jesus replies with the reminder that being his disciple involves suffering. Harris denies that these prophecies were the invention of the early Church. He argues that if this were the case there would be some theological interpretation of the facts mentioned in the prophecy, particularly the exaltation of Jesus would have been mentioned as it was an essential ingredient in the proclamation of the early Church (Acts 2.32, 33, 5.31, 10.42). Harris concludes "It is thus still possible that these passion-resurrection sayings are instances of genuine prophecy: this would adequately account for the detailed nature of the predictions with their references to death by crucifixion and resurrection on the third day. Many, however, exclude such a possibility on *a priori* grounds."[18]

Harris then proceeds to discuss six other passages in the gospels in which Jesus foretells his death and resurrection. The difficulty faced by

Harris is the persistent disbelief of the disciples in face of the very plain and explicit words of Jesus. He argues that the early Church would hardly invent such a failure by the disciples and he suggests that perhaps the prediction about suffering overpowered the prediction about resurrection.

In his study of the formula "received" by Paul, Harris points out that the phrase, "on the third day," is always connected with the resurrection, never with the appearances. The appearances only imply that he rose some time before. "Apart from specific predictions made by Jesus," he tells us, "it is difficult to account adequately for the specific time-note 'on the third day.' "[19] Neither the discovery of the empty tomb, nor the appearances, necessarily imply that Jesus rose on the third day. Once the disciples recognized that his predictions of his passion and resurrection had come to pass, they turned to scripture. This is why the phrase "according to the scripture" was added to the phrase "on the third day."

Harris, with hesitation, accepts the short ending (Mk. 16.8) to Mark's gospel. He sees the gospel as written to emphasize that what Jesus had promised in his work and words was all vindicated by his resurrection. It is also a gospel that constantly emphasizes holy awe as a reaction to God's action in Jesus. This perhaps explains why the gospel ends as it does with the women trembling and astonished.

When we come to Matthew's account, Harris suggests that his special material should not be rejected just because it is clearly apologetic. He sees the encounter on the mountain in Galilee as the climax of Matthew's account. The authority of Jesus, once limited by his earthly messianic vocation now is extended to all creation, his local presence is now, through the resurrection, extended into a universal presence. It will be with his disciples as they teach and baptize until the end of the age.

Harris believes that Luke had an independent Jerusalem tradition about the resurrection and that this explains why his account is different from the others. He suggests that Luke is telling us about another group of women who came to the tomb that morning other than those mentioned by Mark. He points out that Luke places special emphasis on promise and fulfillment. At the beginning and at the end of his gospel, at the birth and at the resurrection of Jesus, the promise of scripture is fulfilled. That promise is fulfilled at Jerusalem. It is the place where Jesus suffers and dies, and the place where raised from the dead he appears, the place where the Spirit-led mission of the Church begins.

As the events in Jerusalem are the climax of Luke's gospel, so the story of Thomas is to be seen as the climax of John's gospel. Jesus accepts Thomas's cry, "My Lord and my God" as a summary of his portrait of Jesus. In a gospel that is built about a series of "signs," the resurrection is to be seen as the final "sign" given by Jesus. Harris sees John's Chapter 21 as an epilogue. The author's aim in adding a Galilean appearance was to record Peter being forgiven by Jesus. He also wanted to rectify a current misunderstanding of some words of Jesus, that is to deny that the approaching death of John meant that the parousia was imminent. Most of all he wanted to include in the gospel the tradition of a Galilean appearance.

Harris gives six arguments for accepting that the tomb of Jesus was found empty. (1) He points out that the tradition is found in all four gospels. (2) The public preaching of the early Church would have been challenged had the tomb not been found empty. (3) Women found the tomb empty at a time they were seen as second-class witnesses. This makes it very unlikely that such a tale would be invented. (4) The claim that Jesus was alive, in those literal days meant, that the tomb had to be empty. (5) The Church soon changed its day of worship from the Sabbath to the first day of the week. (6) No attention was paid to the tomb of Jesus by the early Christians at a time when the tombs of holy men were traditionally venerated. Harris's conclusion then is that "although the empty tomb in itself does not afford conclusive evidence of the resurrection of Jesus, it is not irrelevant in the Christian tradition, for when interpreted, it may serve as the ground for faith in Christ. In addition, it is the presupposition of belief in Jesus' resurrection, a guarantee of the continuity between the earthly Jesus and the risen Lord, and a protection against a spiritualized view of the resurrection."[20]

When he comes to look at the reports of the appearances of Jesus, Harris surveys the various attempts to classify the reports by their form, content and purpose. He tells us that such analysis can be illuminating but it must not be made a basis for questioning the historicity of the material. His conclusion is that "The Resurrection marked his entrance upon a spiritual mode of existence, or to borrow Pauline terminology, his acquisition of a 'spiritual body,' which was both immaterial and invisible yet capable of interaction with the world of time and space."[21]

Harris completes this part of his book with a study of the evidence for and against understanding the resurrection as a verifiable historical event. As we have seen, he is certain that the tomb was found empty and other suggestions, that the women visited the wrong tomb or that the body was removed by the disciples, are found wanting. When he turns to the appearances he argues that, if they were visions, one would have expected the disciples to have been in a psychological or physical condition conducive to such hallucinations. His study of the material shows that this is not the case. He then argues that the resurrection narratives are "self-authenticating." Compared with the later legendary fabrications they are very sober and straightforward. He concludes by pointing to such arguments as the survival of the Church, the transformation of the disciples and the testimony of Christian believers.

Those who reject the historicity of the resurrection, aside from those who rule out the miraculous philosophically, base their objections on the discrepancies in the resurrection material. Harris replies that discrepancies occur in many historical accounts but that does not prove that the central event is not historical. He claims that it is not true to say that a harmonization is impossible and he presents a tentative harmonization of the resurrection events. He lists twenty-one events.

1. After the actual resurrection had taken place, but before dawn, an earthquake occurred, an angel rolled away the stone from the entrance of the tomb; and the guards trembled and fled (Matt. 28.2–4).
2. As Sunday morning was dawning, Mary Magdalene, Mary the mother of James and Joses, and Salome approached the tomb, intending to anoint Jesus with the perfumed oil brought by other women who evidently set out later (see 7.). To their amazement they found the stone rolled away (Matt. 28.1, Mk. 16.1–4, Jn. 20.1).
3. One or more of the women entered the tomb and announced that the body was not there (an inference from Jn. 20.2, where Mary Magdalene does not simply say "The stone has been taken away").
4. Mary Magdalene immediately returned to tell Peter and John that the body had been removed (Jn. 20.2).
5. Mary (the mother of James) and Salome saw an angel (i.e., "a young man" in Mark) inside the tomb who announced the resurrection and directed the women to tell the disciples that Jesus would meet them in Galilee (Matt. 28.5–7, Mk. 16.5–7).
6. These two women returned to the city without greeting anyone on the way, for their holy awe rendered them temporarily speechless (Matt. 28.8, Mk. 16.8).

7. Certain women from Galilee, along with Joanna (cf., Lk. 8.3), arrived at the tomb, carrying perfumed oil to anoint the body of Jesus. They met two "men" (i.e., angels; cf., Lk. 24.4, 23) and then returned to report the angels' message of the resurrection "to the Eleven and to all the rest" (Lk. 24.1–9, 22, 23) who had evidently now gathered together (cf., Matt. 26.56).
8. Meanwhile, informed by Mary Magdalene, Peter and John (and others? Lk. 24.24) ran to the tomb (without meeting Mary and Salome), observed the graveclothes, and returned home (Jn. 20.3–10, and Lk. 24.12, if this is the true text.)
9. Mary Magdalene followed Peter and John to the tomb, saw two angels inside, and then met Jesus (Jn. 20.11–17, cf., Mk. 16.9).
10. Mary Magdalene returned to inform the disciples that Jesus had risen (Jn. 20.18, cf., Mk. 16.10, 11).
11. Mary (the mother of James) and Salome met Jesus and were directed to tell his brethren to go to Galilee (Matt. 28.9, 10).
12. The disciples had now had reports concerning the empty tomb or the Resurrection from three sources (viz., Mary Magdalene; Joanna and the women from Galilee; and Mary (and Salome)), but they refused to believe these reports (Lk. 24.10, 11, cf., Mk. 16.11).
13. During the afternoon Jesus appeared to two disciples on the way to Emmaus. They then returned to Jerusalem to report the appearance to the Eleven and others (Lk. 24.13–35, cf., Mk. 16.12, 13).
14. Jesus appeared to Peter (Lk. 24.34, 1 Cor.15.5).
15. That evening Jesus appeared to the Eleven and others (Lk. 24.33), Thomas being absent (Lk. 24.36–43, Jn. 20.19–23, 1 Cor. 15.5, cf., Mk. 16.14).
16. One week later Jesus appeared to the Eleven, Thomas being present (Jn. 20.26–29).
17. Seven disciples had an encounter with Jesus by the Sea of Tiberias in Galilee (Jn. 21.1–22).
18. The Eleven met Jesus on a mountain in Galilee (Matt. 28.16–20, cf., Mk. 16.15–18).
19. Jesus appeared to more than five hundred brethren (1 Cor. 15.6, Lk. 24.44–49).
20. He appeared to James (1 Cor. 15.7).

21. Immediately before his ascension, Jesus appeared to the Eleven
    near Bethany (Lk. 24.50–52, Acts 1.6–11, 1 Cor. 15.7, cf.,
    Mk. 16.19, 20).[22]

Harris tells us that "The first Christians saw the resurrection as God's
dramatic vindication of the Messiah Israel had rejected (Acts 2.36, 3.14,
15, 4.10, 11). It was also Christ's entrance into his present exalted
state of supreme power and universal dominion (Acts 2.32, 33, 36)
and the inauguration of the new Age, the Age of the Spirit (Acts 2.17,
32, 33)."[23] All this began to happen on that incredible and crowded
first "Lord's Day."

2. Norman Perrin

What can be called the radical approach to the resurrection is best represented in recent times by the work of Norman Perrin. We can see something of his attitude in the little book published just after his death
entitled *The Resurrection According to Matthew, Mark and Luke*.[24] His
approach is to attempt to understand what these three writers are trying
to say when they give their versions of the events at the empty tomb
and, in Matthew and Luke, the appearance of Jesus to the disciples. He
tells us that "the attentive reader will go on to recognize that each of the
gospel writers, the evangelists, has his own particular and distinctive
understanding of the nature of the resurrection of Jesus and that the discrepancies are a consequence of these different understandings."[25] They
expressed their theological convictions in a narrative framework.

Perrin claims that Christians have been mistaken in asking what actually happened in history. What we should ask is what the evangelists
were challenging us to accept or deny by what they had written about
the resurrection. For instance he argues that Mark had a radically different understanding of resurrection because he did not include any resurrection appearances in his gospel.

The passion narrative dominates Mark's gospel in a unique way.
Three times Jesus predicts his passion. The disciples fail to understand
and Jesus tries to correct their misunderstanding. These predictions give
various details about the passion but are "uniformly terse" when they
come to the resurrection. They simply repeat that "after three days he
will rise." Perrin links these passages with the introduction to the trans-

figuration narrative that begins "and after six days" (Mk. 9.2–8). These are the only places in which Mark gives such exact dating. The suggestion then is that we must understand the transfiguration as a symbol of Jesus after his resurrection. Indeed Jesus told the three disciples that they "tell no one what they had seen, until the Son of Man should have risen from the dead." (Mk. 9.9). According to Perrin, Mark, by the careful construction of his gospel, "is telling his readers what it means for him to say that God has raised Jesus from the dead: it means that God has vindicated Jesus out of his death and taken him into heaven to be with Moses and Elijah until the moment, the imminent moment, of his parousia."[26]

This interpretation of the resurrection fits well with Mark's continued emphasis on the end-time, on the return of Jesus, the predictions in Chapter 13 and especially the reply to the high priest "you will see the Son of Man sitting at the right hand of Power, and coming with the clouds of heaven" (Mk. 14.62). People of the time believed that Moses and Elijah had already been taken to live with God in heaven. Elijah, we are told in 2 Kings 2.1–12, was taken to heaven in a whirlwind and an apocalyptic work of the period is entitled *The Assumption of Moses*. Once we put from our minds the appearance stories in the other gospels there is a certain attraction with this suggestion that, in the transfiguration, Jesus is being portrayed proleptically in his post-resurrection state. The suggestion, however, faces various difficulties.

One difficulty, faced by Perrin, is the promise to the women, "But go, tell his disciples and Peter that he is going before you to Galilee; there you will see him" (Mk. 16.7). We are told that in Mark's gospel references to Galilee are not geographical references but primarily refer to the gentile mission. This passage therefore must be understood as a symbolic reference to Jesus leading his disciples in a mission to the gentiles.

Another question that Perrin does not face is why there should be such emphasis on the gentile mission if, for Mark, the resurrection means that Jesus is seated at the right hand of God and that he will soon come in glory at the parousia. Perrin is very clear that Mark sees the disciples failure as total, "The disciples forsake Jesus as a group and flee from the arrest; Peter denies him with oaths while he is on trial; the women, who take on the role of the disciples in this final three-part narrative, fail to deliver the message entrusted to them."[27] It seems strange that the message to these disciples would be that Jesus would lead them in a gentile mission. In his summary Perrin suggests that the reference to Galilee in the "young man's" message for the disciples that the women receive with "trembling and astonishment" is a reference to the site of the parousia.[28] It seems that "Galilee" can symbolically mean several things at once.

Perrin completes his study of Mark's way of understanding the resurrection with an argument from his book, *Jesus and the Language of the Kingdom*.[29] He agrees that the evangelists, particularly Mark, spoke of the coming of the Son of Man as an event in time, yet he suggests Jesus used this language in an existentialist way to refer to "an event which each person would experience in his or her own time."[30] He ends this study by saying, "For me to say 'Jesus is risen' in Markan terms means to say that I experience Jesus as ultimacy in the historicality of my everyday, and that that experience transforms my everydayness as Mark expected the coming of Jesus as Son of Man to transform the world."[31]

When Perrin comes to study Matthew's version of these events he points to the changes Matthew makes in Mark's version. Some of the changes are seen as part of a trend in Matthew to paint a much brighter picture of the disciples. He claims that we can best understand Matthew's theology of the resurrection by a study of the great commission (Matt. 28.16–20). He tells us that "where Mark had understood the reference to Galilee to be symbolic, Matthew understands it as literal and geographical."[32] Perrin studies each part of the commission and concludes that "Whereas Mark understood Jesus to have been taken by God to be with Moses and Elijah in the heavens, whence he would come to exercise his power and authority as Son of Man at his parousia, Matthew understands the risen Jesus as already exercising aspects of that power and authority through the church."[33] The mission of the Church is to make disciples, to baptize, and to teach. While all this takes place, Jesus promises his presence to "the close of the age." For Matthew, therefore, the resurrection means a beginning of a new age, the age of the Church, an age that will end with the parousia. Perrin argues that while Mark wrote for a generation that was still fundamentally Jewish, Matthew's aim was to make the story of Jesus "the foundation myth of Christian origins."[34] Jesus has risen into the Church, and the presence of the risen Lord transforms the believer.

If Matthew's teaching on the resurrection is seen as dominated by a desire to show Jesus setting the Church to its task of "making disciples of all nations," Perrin sees Luke's resurrection reports as dominated by his geographical scheme. Luke sees Jerusalem as a sacred center that is rejected by God and yet it is the place where God himself makes a new beginning. Jesus appears to the disciples at or near Jerusalem. The message to the women is made to refer to a prediction made in Galilee. In the Acts of the Apostles, Luke records the progress of the Christian message from a rejected Jerusalem to the new center of the sacred world, Rome.

Perrin finds that the other two major themes of Luke's gospel have been worked into the major appearance stories. Both the Emmaus story and the appearance in Jerusalem emphasize the interpretation of the scripture as a way to understand the Christ event. The other theme appears in the speech of the risen Jesus in the Jerusalem account. The disciples are promised that they will be "clothed with power from on high" (Lk. 24.49). They are promised that they will be empowered with the same Spirit that had empowered Jesus. Perrin points to the similarity of language between the account of the descent of the Spirit on Jesus at his baptism in Luke's gospel and the account in Acts of the descent of the Spirit on the apostles at Pentecost.

Perrin tells us that Luke, like Matthew, transforms the story of Jesus into a Christian foundation myth: "For Luke the essence of the myth is the fate-laden progress of Jesus to Jerusalem, and of the gospel from Jerusalem to Rome."[35] This is why the resurrection appearances take place in Jerusalem, "The needs of the myth demand it." Luke therefore saw the resurrection as a two-stage event. A human Jesus brought back to life continues his ministry with his disciples. Then he enters into his glory at the Ascension and the disciples begin their ministry. Perrin completes this study by saying "To speak of the resurrection in Lucan terms is to speak of the possibility of a life lived in imitation of the example of Jesus, to speak of the possibility of being moved and empowered by the Spirit of God which is the Spirit of Jesus."[36]

Perrin's attitude to John's teaching on the resurrection can be found in his *New Testament, An Introduction*.[37] Much indebted to his teacher Bultmann, he sees the gospel as a book of signs that presents Jesus as a kind of hellenistic "divine man." Here miracles induce faith, whereas in the synoptics, faith results in miracles.

The appearances in John Chapter 20 put a major emphasis on the theme put forward in Chapter 6.62, 63 and Chapter 16.7–11, passages that speak of the eventual return of Jesus to the heavenly realm so that his spiritual presence with the believer will be possible. Jesus tells

Mary Magdalene that he is about to ascend (Jn. 20.17). The next appearance and that made to Thomas dramatize what is now possible for all who accept Jesus. His Spirit, his breath, will bring all believers to say "My Lord and my God" (Jn. 20.28).

The original end to the gospel (Jn. 20.30, 31) sums up the purpose of the gospel. Perrin believes that Chapter 21 was added by another hand, someone with ecclesiastical concerns. The writer made four points. He confirmed the tradition of an appearance in Galilee. He emphasized the place of the eucharist in Church life. He testified to the restoration of Peter. He identified the disciple Jesus loved as the author of the gospel.

When Perrin comes to consider 1 Corinthians 15.3–7 he tells us that the empty tomb tradition is comparatively late and is probably "a way of saying 'Jesus is risen' rather then a description of an aspect of the event itself."[38] Because Paul lists himself among those to whom the risen Christ has appeared, Paul's attitude, shown in passages such as 1 Corinthians 15.3–7, Galatians 1.15, 16, 1 Corinthians 9.1, 2 and Philippians 3.7–11, is very important. In these passages Paul usually seems to be arguing that his own experience of Jesus is to be equated with that of Peter and the others. Perrin suggests that the "intensive theological motivation" of the evangelists Matthew and Luke can account for the difficulty in reconciling their accounts with Paul's list.[39]

Perrin concludes that all that can be said from Paul's references to the resurrection appearances is that those listed had in some way been granted a vision "which convinced them that God had vindicated Jesus out of his death, and that therefore the death of Jesus was by no means the end of the impact of Jesus upon their lives and upon the world in which they lived. Very much to the contrary, since Jesus as risen commissioned them to new tasks and to new responsibilities."[40]

This is more than can be said for the Gospel narratives for each of them has a different purpose when they come to speak of the resurrection. Mark is "attempting to convince his readers that they can experience the ultimacy of God in the concreteness, the historicality of everyday existence."[41] Matthew is attempting to convince his readers that the Church is the vehicle of salvation. Luke is attempting to convince his readers that Jesus lived as the first Christian and that his spirit empowers those who would imitate him. John gives us dramatizations of the power of Jesus enthroned at the right hand of God.

For Perrin, therefore, all we can know about the resurrection is de-

pendent on the reports in the writings of Paul, and from his reports all
we can tell is that some followers of Jesus were in some way granted a
vision of the risen Lord.

3. Willi Marxsen

The best known of those who concentrate their study on the reports of
the resurrection and then work back from those reports to the ministry of
Jesus is Willi Marxsen in his book *The Resurrection of Jesus of
Nazareth*.[42] The title of the book tells us of Marxsen's intent, a study of
the resurrection that will lead to Jesus, the man of Nazareth.

Marxsen begins with "the later texts of the resurrection of Jesus"
(the Apostles' Creed and the four gospels) and shows that despite many
disagreements there are common themes. Although the risen "body" of
Jesus may be spoken of in different terms and in different ways, the
point is always made that the Jesus seen by the disciples was the same
Jesus who had been crucified. At various times the disciples show doubt
but that doubt is soon overcome, as we see most clearly in the Thomas
story.

Marxsen points out that all these accounts, in spite of great differences in detail, represent the Easter happenings as a sequence of events.
One way of understanding the variations in the lists of incidents would
be to suggest that the individual evangelists only reported selected parts
of the Easter events and that our task is therefore that of harmonizing
their reports. He calls this solution "completely untenable." His own
solution is to suggest that, "the evangelists, working from the existing
units of tradition, ask themselves in what order the Easter events can
have taken place. Since there was no uniform tradition on this point in
the primitive church, each evangelist did the best he could to establish
the order."[43] What each evangelist wanted to say, in his own way, was,
"the activity of Jesus goes on." "The conclusions of the different
works are therefore designed to explain why what we have been told
about the past (with respect to Jesus' words and works) is not a thing of
the past at all, but is vitally relevant to the present."[44] Faith now is determined by what Jesus said and did in the past. The point that all the
evangelists make is that his cause goes on. The fact that it does go on is
always attributed to a new commission by Jesus but at the time the
evangelists were writing there were various ideas about just how this
new commission was delivered, "the mode of the resurrection was not

an article of faith and was not part of a universal Christian conviction."[45]

Marxsen's next step is to attempt to go behind the gospels to find the pre-gospel traditions. He tells us that Paul does not give us his list of the Church leadership in 1 Corinthians 15 because they were all witnesses of the resurrection, the point that Paul was trying to make was that they were all people who had proclaimed the resurrection. It is not that they witnessed the resurrection itself. Their experience is described as "seeing" Jesus. Together they gave witness to post-resurrection appearances. He makes this distinction on the basis of verse 11 ("Whether then it was I or they, so we preach and so you believed"). Paul's list supports Marxsen's conclusions drawn from his study of the later texts that the first appearance was to Peter and then afterwards there was an appearance to the twelve. No further comparisons are possible.

Marxsen asks why the formula used by Paul in 1 Corinthians 15 speaks about the twelve when the texts speak about appearances to the eleven. According to Luke it was only after the Ascension that the election of Matthias took place. The election could not have taken place before the appearance to Peter because at that time there was no need for such an election. Marxsen then concludes that "If it took place immediately afterwards, then the group of twelve owed its existence at least to the appearance to Peter. It did not owe its existence to the appearance to the twelve."[46] He concedes that the group may have later had an appearance experience but it was only the appearance to Peter that was "constitutive."

If we agree that the faith of the twelve had its origin, not in a personal appearance of Jesus but solely in an appearance to Peter ("The Lord has risen indeed and has appeared to Simon" (Luke 24.34)), then many of the problems with Paul's formula disappear. We can then see that the list is not a report of a number of appearances. The formula becomes a list of the leadership groups in the early Church. Paul feels that he has a rightful claim to membership in these groups who all share the faith that they have "seen" Jesus. As Marxsen puts it, "Why are we told that all these different groups experienced an appearance of Jesus? What is the point of the narrative? I think it is this: their faith, the manifold functions which they exercised, are all in the ultimate resort based on the first appearance to Peter. They are all summed up in this appearance."[47] Peter's experience, Peter's vision, Peter's seeing Jesus, resulted in mission as his faith led others to faith.

After a study of the "vision" of Paul and his teaching about that experience, Marxsen concludes that Paul never uses that experience as factual evidence for the resurrection. The content of his preaching about the resurrection does not include the way in which that resurrection occurred. Jesus can be experienced as "alive" in faith, but faith cannot tell how he came to be alive, how it is to be understood as an historical event. This is why Paul can at times speak of the event that brought him to faith as a "revealing" (Gal. 1.15–17) and later as a "seeing" (1 Cor. 9.1f, 15.8).

What Marxsen calls the "miracle of the resurrection" is that the faith that Jesus called people to share before the crucifixion was still alive. To speak of the resurrection, therefore, is to say that "God endorsed Jesus as the person that he was."[48] Just as we cannot tell how an individual arrives at faith, so we cannot tell how Peter arrived at faith. The how is of no great importance. What is important is that the faith that Jesus taught is still alive, it has risen from death.

Marxsen has not always taken this position. In an earlier essay entitled *The Resurrection of Jesus as a Historical and Theological Problem*,[49] he tried to show that it was the "appearances" of Jesus that were the beginning point of faith. He seems to have rejected this understanding because it could suggest that faith could be seen as a human "work" and not as the free gift of God.

It is very difficult to tell just what Marxsen means when he tells us that "the activity of Jesus goes on." He seems to reduce the appearance stories and the empty tomb narratives merely to imaginative ways of saying that the faith of Jesus is still alive. In a way, he builds his whole account of the resurrection on what happened to Peter. Yet it is hard to tell precisely what he means when he tells us that Jesus appeared to Peter. At times he seems to mean that Jesus literally appeared, as Marxsen puts it, "The cause of Jesus goes on beyond Good Friday—in a miraculous way, it must be added. And the fact that it goes on is always due to a new emergence and intervention of Jesus, to a new commission."[50] This can mean that the resurrection is an event in the life of Jesus, that he is the active subject who has imparted his presence to Peter. On the other hand, there are passages that suggest that what the resurrection means is that the activity and teaching that Jesus began have been taken up and continued by his disciples. Marxsen refers to a German hymn that goes, "Still he comes today"—in which both elements are stressed: it is really *he* who comes; and *he* really comes *today*—"and what comes today is the same thing that Jesus of Nazareth brought."[51] Marxsen can at times suggest that what we call the resurrection makes little difference, "The faith which Peter held after the death of Jesus, a faith into which others were then drawn (and it is only their statements which are available to us) and the faith into which these people called yet others—this faith did not differ in substance from the faith to which Jesus of Nazareth called men."[52] In another passage he tells us that "Since the subject is always the faith brought by the earthly Jesus, Jesus alone is the indispensable factor. Jesus is dead. But his offer has not thereby lost its validity. That fact was experienced at the time and it can equally well be experienced today."[53]

If, for Marxsen, resurrection means that faith exists, then aside from his emphasis on Peter, his teaching is little different from Bultmann's. It is a position that can only be held by rejecting what the New Testament (for example, 1 Cor. 6.14) seems to say and what Christian tradition has taught down the ages. If on the other hand, we understand Marxsen to speak of the identity of Jesus enduring, his reluctance to suggest what actually happened to Peter and his negative attitude to the historicity of the narratives makes it difficult to understand what he calls "the address of Jesus."[54]

Marxsen tells us that Peter and the other disciples felt a call to live the life Jesus lived and they came to that faith after the crucifixion. He describes that faith in these words, "during his earthly lifetime Jesus pronounced the forgiveness of sins to men in the name of God. He demanded that they commit their lives entirely to God, that they should really take no thought for the morrow. He demanded of them that they should put themselves entirely at the service of their neighbor. He demanded of them that they risk their lives—and that meant giving up any attempt to assert themselves. He demanded of them that they work for peace even where it was dangerous, humanly speaking, because it could mean the relinquishing of one's own rights. And he promised people that in fulfilling this demand they would find true life, life with God."[55] The disciples then proclaimed their new, or perhaps better, their renewed faith with the words "Jesus is risen" Marxsen tells us that they used this expression because "If (in whatever way) a man came to believe in Jesus after Good Friday, he knew himself to be called to faith by the same Jesus who performed an earthly ministry, who called men to faith, and who died on the cross. But if this Jesus was still able to call men to faith (and that he was able was clear from the reality of the believer's own faith) then it followed that he was not dead but alive. And that could be expressed by saying: 'He is risen.' "[56]

Perhaps the experience of faith can be expressed by the words "He is risen," but it does seem to be a strange way of expressing the reality of a believer's faith in Jesus of Nazareth. As far as we can tell, the disciples may have expected a resurrection at the last day, but there is little in the story of Jesus to prepare them for the resurrection of a single individual. Marxsen does not suggest that the disciples had accepted the detailed prophecies of the resurrection that the evangelist put on the lips of Jesus. It seems difficult to follow Marxsen when he suggests that people continued to believe in Jesus and that therefore "He is risen" when the New Testament calls on people to believe in Jesus because "He is risen."

Marxsen argues that the resurrection was only one of the ways in which the New Testament expresses the new reality of faith. The Epistle to the Hebrews only alludes to the resurrection while it speaks of the exalted Jesus seated at the right hand of God. That same theme is found in the pre-Pauline hymn to Christ (Phil. 2.5–11). He suggests that the idea of exaltation might lie behind the scene on the mountain at the end of Matthew's gospel. He also points to the same theme in 1 Timothy 3.16 and in the Gospel of John (7.33, 12.32). Marxsen tells us that exaltation was the earlier way, the primary way of saying that the activity of Jesus continues before the idea of resurrection won ascendancy.

Marxsen's account certainly makes us look at the familiar texts of the resurrection in a new light, but in the end he fails to explain how faith arose or why it took the form it did. He saw the resurrection texts as pointing to Jesus of Nazareth. Let us now turn to those who would look at the life of Jesus of Nazareth to understand the resurrection texts.

4. Peter Carnley

Peter Carnley, in *The Structure of Resurrection Belief,*[57] is an excellent example of those who tend to look forward from the life and ministry of Jesus to explain and interpret the resurrection. After a survey of the more important recent studies of the resurrection under the Chapter headings "The Resurrection as a Historical Event" (Westcott and Pannenberg), "The Resurrection as an Eschatological Event" (Barth and Bultmann), and "The Resurrection as a Non-Event" (Marxsen and Cupitt), Carnley comes to his own interpretation. He suggests that his study of the difficulties in the historical approach shows that our real conviction about the resurrection comes from our own present encounter with the glorified Jesus. Yet, "most attempts to appeal to the believer's present experience of the raised Christ, in order to clarify and validate the historical account of the first appearances, have run into the difficulty that the raised Christ tends to become so elusive as to recede from view and all but disappear."[58] His suggestion is that with our own understanding of the risen Christ as our base, we look at what the first Christians claimed to have experienced or encountered after the crucifixion. We must ask what it was that led those first Christians to their firm conviction that Jesus had been raised. What exactly were they claiming when they gave us their accounts of the resurrection? Carnley then sets out on his task of discovering the nature of the appearance and presence of the raised Christ.

The first point Carnley makes is that the central claim of 1 Corinthians 15 and the gospel narratives is that "seeing Jesus" is the basis of the affirmation of resurrection belief. It was this experience that "provided the experiential ground for the inference that Jesus had been raised in the tomb and also for theological speculation concerning the heavenly place where Jesus had gone and whence he had appeared."[59] He suggests that it is unfortunate that "seeing" Jesus has tended to be interpreted in either the ordinary sense of seeing something with one's eyes or in the more intellectual sense of seeing something of the truth about the historical Jesus. He tells us that both these views are mistaken and that the truth lies somewhere between the ordinary and the intellectual use of the word. Although the word is used in the Septuagint to describe a religious revelation, it is also used in that translation in the ordinary literal sense of seeing.

The next step is a study of the reports of those who have claimed to "see" the risen Christ. Carnley tells us that Paul speaks of the resurrection in terms of a "spiritual body" (Phil. 1.22–24, 1 Cor. 15.50, 2 Cor. 5.1f). He suggests that the reason Paul does not speak of the "empty tomb" is that he sees the raised Christ as having a glorified "spiritual body." His "Damascus Road" experience then must have been some kind of "heavenly vision." In the gospel appearances the raised Christ appears in a clear and physical way in Luke and John yet even there he vanishes from sight and passes through walls. In Matthew Jesus speaks as the already exalted Christ who appears "from heaven." His study leads Carnley to conclude that whatever was "seen" appeared "from heaven" and therefore any attempt to understand "seeing" in the ordinary way is "extremely precarious."[60] Whether we call the Easter appearances "objective" or "subjective" visions, the first disciples interpreted them as signs of the heavenly presence of Christ. This tradition of "heavenly visions" continues, it is the ground of our faith just as it was the ground of the faith of those first disciples. As Carnley puts it "The requisite and necessary additional empirical evidence of the fact that Jesus was raised is the experience of his continuing presence as Spirit."[61]

The experience of those first disciples and our experience today is that the "Spirit," is the raised and exalted Christ. The early Christians used various terms, Spirit, Holy Spirit, God's Spirit, the Spirit of Christ, but all these terms referred to the same reality, the reality of the Easter experience. This experience can be understood as something that can be "seen", or something that can be "known," or both.

The next problem Carnley must face is this: if the resurrection faith is a present experience, how is it possible to recognize this "presence" as the presence of Jesus. He tells us that what he calls the "cognitive nucleus" of Easter faith, this experience of the Spirit includes the memory of the historical Jesus. This "nucleus" has two types of memory. On the one hand there are the facts about Jesus, the details the disciples remembered, what we can gather from historical research. On the other hand there is the knowledge of Jesus himself from the memory of the disciples and the Church. Carnley makes use of a philosophical distinction between the various kinds of "remembering." There is "perceptual" memory which we can equate with our memory of Jesus himself. There is "factual" memory which consists of various facts about Jesus. Perceptual memory is dependent on factual memory but it is separate from factual memory. The Church's perceptual memory of Jesus is of "a man, a human person, who died on the cross, and who exhibited a distinctive quality of character and that this quality of character can be expressed in terms of the concept of *agape*."[62] This memory of Jesus is "presupposed when, in Easter faith, the Church makes claims to recognize *His* living presence."[63] Unless the Church first "remembers Jesus," it cannot recognize and identify the Spirit of its own corporate life as the "Spirit" or the "presence" of Jesus. The Church therefore remembers Jesus so that it may recognize and identify its religious experience as the "presence" or "Spirit" of Jesus. Remembering and knowing are interrelated but separate. Jesus is known as present because he is remembered by the Church. Carnley would not agree that the reverse is also true.

Carnley tells us that this emphasis on the distinction between "remembering" and "knowing" makes his contribution different from what he calls the "reductionist" theologians who claim that the disciples simply "saw" Jesus in a new and unexpected way after the crucifixion. He feels that resurrection faith is more than a shared memory. It affirms that the Jesus remembered is also the Jesus that was "seen" as a heavenly, exalted presence after the crucifixion, "In the specific case of the Easter faith the empirically given reality which is the object of faith is identified as 'the Spirit or presence of Jesus.' This judgement is only possible, however, because the proper name 'Jesus' and the criteria for its correct use have been learned in the context of the believer's acquaintance with the Church understood as a linguistic community whose processes of proclamation and catechesis equipped the believer with the ability to identify the 'presence of Christ' by bringing a concretely given element of religious experience under an interpretive name."[64] It is the Church then that "remembers Jesus" and it is the Church that also "knows his living presence." The Lord's Supper can be seen as a time of "remembering Jesus" and yet it is also a time when the Church "knows" Jesus. Carnley tells us "Once again the eucharist is an occasion for knowing Jesus: his living presence is known in the breaking of bread. The liturgy of the eucharist indeed is both a remembering of the human Jesus and the receiving and communing with the divine Lord as Spirit."[65]

"Remembering" and "knowing" cannot be separated. Memory can be informed by the Spirit, the Spirit can be informed by memory. Nor does it follow that "memory" precedes "knowing." "Knowing" may precede "remembering" when the Spirit's presence is identified as the Spirit of Christ. Carnley suggests that this is the way we should understand the gospels where the disciples are portrayed as only having a clear memory of Jesus after they recognized his living presence, as for example, in Luke 24.8 when "they remembered his words." In the experience of the Spirit of Christ we come to know the presence of that heavenly and divine *agape* love, eternal and infinite, which we "remember" as having been defined by the life and death of Jesus. At times the resurrection reports seem to be historical, others seem to be imaginative ways of making a theological statement. Therefore the problem of historicity cannot be resolved. The Easter stories are "useful" in so far as they "direct our attention to the reality of the raised Christ, whose presence may, even today, be known by acquaintance."[66]

Carnley enters into discussion with a great number of scholars in an attempt to combine the thinking of those who see the resurrection as a "memory" of the human Jesus with those who understand the resurrection as a "knowing" of the divine Christ. A "knowing" that brings our salvation. He uses the "Spirit," always written with a capital, to connect these two concepts. Yet he fails to convince us that our experience of the presence of Christ today is anything like the presence of the risen Christ that is described in so many different ways in the New Testament reports. In these reports it is not the "Spirit" that is spoken of, it is Jesus, the Christ, who appears. We may well have a religious, mystical experience of the "Spirit" which we may identify as a meeting with the risen Christ but it is difficult to imagine that such an experience is what the gospels describe as "seeing" Jesus.

5. Conclusion

It is not too difficult to see the problems we face if we accept either of the more extreme positions of theologians who would explain the resurrection. If we accept the reports as those that tell of a historical event in literal language, aside from the difficulties imposed in harmonizing the reports, we have to face the problem of doing justice to the unique, transcendent quality of the appearances. The resurrection cannot be just a resuscitation and a resumption by Jesus of his former life. The raised Jesus, his body glorified and transformed is seen by the disciples and then by the Church as a new creation, a new revelation.

On the other hand, when we turn to the radical theologians we find that we are asked to base our entire faith on the earthly life of Jesus. What really happened after his death, we are told, is that his disciples thought about the events they had experienced, contemplated the scriptures, accepted God's forgiveness and then explained that experience in the words "The Lord is risen." As Perrin put it, "in some way" they were granted a vision but that vision came because of the faith that they already had in Jesus. Therefore the real Easter event is the coming to faith itself rather than something to which people responded with faith. Talk about Jesus being alive then means that the things he stood for in this life are still alive, his example is before us.

Those who attempt to show that the truth of the resurrection must come somewhere between these two extremes seem better able to inspire our confidence. Marxsen tells us that resurrection faith calls us to a commitment to Jesus, the Man from Nazareth. When we study the resurrection events we are led to see them as expressions of a commitment to that faith. This is the miracle of the resurrection. We are led to look back to that life, as the disciples looked back, and then commit ourselves to Jesus of Nazareth as Peter and then the disciples committed themselves when they proclaimed that the activity of Jesus continues for "He is risen from the dead."

Carnley attempts to proceed in the other direction. He attempts to show how the life of Jesus "remembered" resulted in the disciples "knowing" the presence of Jesus. The experience of the "Spirit" led the disciples, and can lead us to "remember" Jesus and "know" that we are in his presence, in the presence of the Spirit of Jesus. Perhaps "remembering" and "knowing" can be brought together in another, more simple way, than that suggested by Carnley.

Part Three

Training the Twelve

Jesus believed that the kingdom of God was at hand (Mk. 1.15). He believed that he had been called by God to announce and to prepare for the new age just as John the Baptist had prepared the way for Jesus (Mk. 9.12, 13, Matt. 17.10–12). On many occasions Jesus states that he does not know, nor does anyone know, when the kingdom will come (Matt. 24.36, 42, 25.13, Mk. 13.32, 33, 35, Lk. 12.40). Yet it seems that Jesus expected the kingdom to come quickly (Matt. 16.28, 24.34, Mk. 9.1, 13.30, Lk. 9.27, 21.23).

In preparation for the coming of God's kingdom, Jesus chose twelve men to "be with him" (Mk. 3.14) for he believed that the time was at hand when this group would "sit on twelve thrones, judging the twelve tribes of Israel" (Matt. 19.28). It is difficult to believe that the early Church would invent this saying, or others like it, in which the one who betrayed Jesus is promised that he will be among those who will sit on thrones judging Israel. Matthew follows this passage with a parable from his special source, the story of the Laborers in the Vineyard. Perhaps this parable was part of the disciples training as it tells of divine generosity. The theme of judgement appears again in the same chapter when Matthew has the mother of James and John, instead of James and John themselves as in Mark, ask that her sons be given privileged positions sitting on thrones on either side of Jesus when the kingdom had come (Matt. 20.20–23). Luke has a similar passage. His setting is the last supper and a discussion about suffering service. Jesus tells the disciples "as my Father appointed about a kingdom for me, so do I appoint for you, that you may eat and drink at my table in my kingdom and sit

on thrones judging the twelve tribes of Israel" (Lk. 22.29, 30). The
same theme appears in the book of Revelation where "one like the Son
of Man" tells the Church of Laodicea that "Behold, I stand at the door
and knock; if any one hears my voice and opens the door, I will come
into him and eat with him and he with me. He who conquers, I will
grant him to sit with me on my throne, as I myself conquered and sat
down with my Father on his throne" (Rev. 3.20, 21).

We will argue in these chapters that most of the ministry of Jesus consisted of the training and preparation of this small group. Indeed it
seems likely that the very texts that we have about the life of Jesus come
directly from that training. The gospels are not "eye-witness" accounts
gathered by later writers. They should be seen as edited collections of
the oral teaching of Jesus, which was received, remembered and handed
down by the twelve. For many years the gospels have been understood
as the literary creation of the early Church. The priority of Mark and the
source called "Q" have been accepted by a general consensus. Re-
cently however, the importance of the oral tradition, first emphasized
by Swedish scholars, has again been applied to gospel criticism. It has
been pointed out that in oriental literature the living tradition dominated. Village reciters of traditional tales have been found to have an
immense capacity. Old Testament traditions were applied to gospel criticism by Harald Riesenfeld who concluded that the oral teaching of
Jesus was the direct source of the Gospel tradition.[67] Birger Gerhardsson, in his book *The Origins of the Gospel Traditions,* suggests
that Jesus, like the rabbis of the time, used memorization as a training
technique.[68] We are told that the disciples called Jesus "Rabbi" (e.g.,
Jn. 1.38, 49) or "Teacher" (e.g., Mk. 4.35f, 5.35f, par.), even in
the midst of the storm on the lake. Much of the recent study of the gospels has centered about a renewed interest in the connection between the
training of the twelve and the written works that we have today. Bo
Reicke tells us that the oral traditions must have been the link between
Jesus and our written material.[69] He suggests that what he calls the
"context-parallel triple units" can be traced back to the celebration of
baptism and eucharist in the early Church. We suggest that the common
tradition goes back further, to a common source, the training of the disciples. Luke referred to these living traditions in his prologue, when he
said he would base his report on what original eyewitnesses and servants of the word had delivered to him as tradition (Lk. 1.2). The other
gospel writers would have also used such traditions. Reicke suggests
that it is possible by internal analysis of the entire synoptic material to

show how these living traditions were kept in various regions of the land to be handed down to the gospel writers.[70]

The small group formed by Jesus memorized his words as he trained them for their role in the kingdom. The Sermon on the Mount, and the parables of Jesus then must be seen as addressed, at first, to the twelve. We will suggest that they were asked to face the possibility of martyrdom when they were asked to "carry their cross." They were taught a life of prayer, taught to live in the presence of the "Father." They were trained to heal the sick and to exorcise demons. All through this training they shared in a special time together, a daily meal at which Jesus broke bread in the way he expected his body to be broken in crucifixion.

Many of the incidents in the life of Jesus must therefore be seen as incidents that primarily involved that small group about Jesus. We tend to picture great crowds about Jesus most of the time because that is what the evangelists want us to believe. When we look more closely we find that often a narrative that is connected with a crowd in one gospel has been connected with the disciples in another. For instance, the explanation of the parable of the Sower and the parables of the Lamp, the Measure and the Mustard Seed in Mark are addressed to "those who were about him with the twelve" (Mk. 4.10), in the absence of the crowd. In Matthew "all this Jesus said to the crowds in parables; indeed he said nothing to them without a parable" (Matt. 13.34). In Luke, as far as we can tell, these passages are addressed to the disciples alone. A similar difference appears in the story of the storm on the lake. In Luke, Jesus simply suggests to the disciples that they cross the lake (Lk. 8.22). In Matthew, when "Jesus saw great crowds around him, he gave orders to go to the other side" (Matt. 8.18). In Mark they cross "leaving the crowd" (Mk. 4.35). As introduction to the saying of Jesus on discipleship, Mark has "he called to him the multitude with his disciples" (Mk. 8.34), Matthew has "Then Jesus told his disciples" (Matt. 16.24), while Luke has "and he said to all" (Lk. 9.23) at a time when he was alone with the twelve.

Mark seems to go out of his way to contrast the behavior of the crowds with that of the disciples. The crowd understands and "were all amazed and glorified God, saying 'We never saw anything like this' " (Mk. 2.12). Yet Mark has the quotation from Isaiah (Mk. 4.12) followed by a statement telling us of the incomprehension of the disciples. This theme continues through Mark's gospel. The disciples constantly fail to understand and finally they all desert Jesus although Mark pictures Jesus always surrounded by a friendly crowd that follows him everywhere, even into the desert (Mk. 6.34). He always teaches this crowd (Mk. 9.15, 11.18). He has pity on them (Mk. 6.34, 8.6, 12). The crowds are amazed by what they see and hear (Mk. 9.15, 11.18). They lead Jesus to "teach them many things" (Mk. 6.34). Mark contrasts the attitude of the crowd with that of the family and friends of Jesus (Mk. 3.20, 21, 3.31–35). Mark tells us that Jesus saw the crowd sitting about him as his family. Mark seems to have had a special purpose in emphasizing the importance of the crowds in the ministry of Jesus.[71] Perhaps we find a better perspective in John's gospel where crowds are only mentioned three times (Jn. 5.13, 6.2, 12.12–19).

We usually picture the triumphal entry as an event that was important to many of the people of Jerusalem. Matthew tells us that as Jesus began his ride into the city "Most of the crowd spread their garments on the road, and others cut branches from the trees and spread them on the road. And the crowd that went before him and that followed shouted 'Hosanna to the Son of David' "(Matt. 21.8, 9). Then when Jesus actually came into the city "all the city was stirred" (Matt. 21.10). In John's gospel it is the crowds that initiate the event. A "great crowd" heard that Jesus was coming to Jerusalem "So they took branches of palm trees and went out to meet him" (Jn. 12.13). They even hail him as "King of Israel." When this happens Jesus takes the occasion to act out the prophecy in Zechariah 9.9. Yet John tells us "His disciples did not understand this at first; but when Jesus was glorified, then they remembered that this had been written of him" (Jn. 12.16). The passage ends with the Pharisees in despair for "all the world has gone after him" (Jn. 12.19). It is only in Matthew and John that the claim to be king is explicit (Matt. 21.9, Jn. 12.13). Luke, in his report of the triumphal entry is much more conservative. It is the two disciples who have been sent to fetch the colt who spread their garments on the colt and throw them on the road (Lk. 19.35, 36). As they begin the descent of the Mount of Olives it is the "whole multitude of disciples" that begins to rejoice. The passage ends with the Pharisees asking Jesus to rebuke the disciples for what they have said (Lk. 19.39). Mark is even more restrictive. Indeed, if the other evangelists who wrote later had not expanded their accounts to include greater and greater numbers we might assume that the triumphal entry was a quiet affair. In Mark it is something that involves Jesus and the disciples. In Mark the two disciples bring the colt to Jesus and throw their garments on the animal. "And many" (disciples), spread their garments on the road. "And others" spread leafy branches (Mk. 11.8). There is no mention of any response from the people of Jerusalem or of any questions by the Pharisees. Mark tells us that Jesus "entered Jerusalem and went into the Temple; and when he had looked around at everything, as it was already late, he went out to Bethany with the twelve" (Mk. 11.11).

One way to understand the diversity of these accounts is to suppose that Jesus and the twelve understood that he was entering Jerusalem as a king, in fulfillment of the prophecy in Zechariah but that there was no large public involvement in the event. Mark's account is therefore close to what actually happened.

If the entry had involved "all the city" and Jesus had been proclaimed King or Messiah, the Romans would have taken action. They were not slow to deal with sedition. There would have been no need for a Jewish trial. There would be no need to explain the fickleness of the crowd that one day hailed Jesus as King and several days later cried "crucify him."[72]

The triumphal entry, like so much of the New Testament story, primarily involved Jesus and the twelve. There were crowds that came to Jesus, attracted by his teaching and more often by his miracles of healing and exorcism. Yet Jesus made no attempt to organize the crowds. He did not set up a clinic or a hospice. We have no record that, when he went from Galilee to Jerusalem, there remained a continuing body of followers in Galilee. It almost seems that he used the crowds as a means of training his small group. He made no attempt to form his own organization, his only organization was the twelve. He does not seem to have spent his time in helping the "sinners" he met to return to the Jewish community. There is little evidence to suggest that he expected them to repent, make restitution, perform the required sacrifice at the Temple and return to community life.[73] As far as we can tell, Jesus made no attempt to reach all of Israel with his preaching. Most of his ministry was centered on a very small area on the Galilean shore. Jesus did not have a practical strategy to "bring" the end-time. He did not plan to raise rebellion. This is why his disciples were ignored when Jesus came to crucifixion. He was certain that God would bring the end; the kingdom of God would soon come. It was his ministry to prepare for that day by training the small group that would rule with him in God's kingdom. Let us consider some of these suggestions as we study the training of the twelve disciples.

1. The Disciples

How do we see the ministry of Jesus? Do we not tend to follow the pattern established by our own experience of a modern day evangelist? We see Jesus coming "into Galilee, preaching the gospel of God" with the result that "his fame spread everywhere throughout all the surrounding region of Galilee" (Mk. 1.14, 28). We see Paul and other evangelists following this pattern in the Acts of the Apostles. A leader would gather a group or a team who would proceed to evangelize a given area, in much the way Mark describes Jesus beginning his work in Galilee, or much in the way an evangelist in our time would begin to work in any community.

We have been so conditioned by our own experience, and by the gospels themselves to see Jesus' ministry in this way, that we fail to see a very different pattern until we take a closer look. That pattern in modern dress would be more akin to a religious leader who gathers a group of students and takes them day after day to live among the poor, the hungry, the diseased of society. Such a group would live where they could, on occasion accepting the hospitality of the more wealthy members of society but normally sharing the life of those who live in shelters for the homeless, who eat in soup kitchens and drop-in centers for the mentally ill. The main focus of such a group's life, however, would not be on these institutions but on the training they received from the religious leader as they encountered and confronted the members of these various social groups.

We can see this pattern in the sayings of Jesus that have been preserved in the gospels. It is difficult to imagine how these sayings could have been preserved if they were not the actual words of Jesus because they certainly do not fit the circumstances of the early Church at the time the gospels were written. The call of discipleship from Jesus meant giving up the identity that normally comes with a home, a family, a trade and possessions. One who would follow him is told, "Foxes have holes and the birds of the air have nests, but the Son of Man has nowhere to lay his head" (Matt. 8.20). The renunciation of a fixed location includes breaking with one's family obligations. In the next passage in Matthew another disciple asks, "Lord, let me first go and bury my father" but Jesus tells him to "leave the dead to bury their own dead" (Matt. 8.21, 22). One condition of discipleship is hating one's own father and mother, wife and children, brothers and sisters (Lk. 14.26). Indeed it is important for the sake of the kingdom of heaven to be as a eunuch (Matt. 19.12). This behavior seemed very strange to family members. When the family of Jesus came to see him he would not go out to greet them but said to those about him, "Who are my mother and my brothers. Whoever does the will of God is my brother and sister and mother" (Mk. 3.34, 35). Family and possessions seem to be what is in Peter's mind when he says, "Lo, we have left everything and followed you" (Mk. 10.28). The renunciation of family and trade also meant the renunciation of wealth and property. The story of the rich young ruler shows that this is part of full discipleship (Mk. 10.17–31). If someone wants your cloak, give him your coat as well (Lk. 6.29). If someone wants your goods, give them to him and do not ask for them again (Lk. 6.30). The treasures that matter are in heaven, not on earth (Matt. 6.19–21). A camel can go through the eye of a needle more easily than a rich man can enter the kingdom of God (Mk. 10.25).

The passage in the Sermon on the Mount that begins "Do not be anxious" (Matt. 6.25) takes on new meaning when we see it as describing the life-style that the disciples were expected to follow. We see that life-style set out most clearly when, as part of their training, the disciples were sent out two by two (Lk. 6.25–28). They are to accept hospitality when it is offered (Lk. 10.5–7), but otherwise they are homeless (Lk. 9.4). There is no provision for meals, they are forbidden to take bread, or money, or a wallet (Lk. 9.3). They are not allowed shoes (Matt. 10.10) or an extra coat (Mk. 6.9). The disciples are told to "Ask and it will be given you; seek and you will find; knock and it will be opened unto you" (Lk. 11.9). There must have been times when they went hungry. If a house refuses to receive them they are told to "shake off the dust that is on your feet for a testimony against them" (Mk. 6.11). The story of the disciples gleaning the fields on the Sabbath probably reflects the experience of just such a rebuff. Perhaps they often went hungry because no one would receive them. They must have often been chased away. A passage in Matthew 10.23 says, "when they persecute you in one town, flee to the next; for truly I say to you, you will not have gone through all the towns of Israel before the Son of Man comes."

This was a training program. It was not door to door or village to village evangelism. They were not expected to cover the whole land. To encourage them, Jesus points to the important place they have in God's plan, "Blessed are you when men revile you and persecute you and utter all kinds of evil against you falsely on my account. Rejoice and be glad, for your reward is great in heaven, for so men persecuted the prophets who were before you" (Matt. 5.11, 12). They were to face this persecution without protection. They had renounced family, friends, possessions. They were men of "no fixed abode." When Mark came to tell his version of the mission of the twelve he found it hard to believe that they were sent out without purse, staff or even shoes (Mk. 6.8, 9). Matthew (10.10) and Luke (9.3) are probably more correct with their rigid prohibitions. By their actions they were to make clear to all that they would not resist evil, that they would offer the left cheek if they were struck on the right (Matt. 5.38f), that they would go two miles if they were pressed into service for one mile (Matt. 5.41). They were sent "as sheep in the midst of wolves" (Matt. 10.16). Even when they were taken to the authorities to be flogged they were not to concern themselves with a defence (Matt. 10.17f). If possible they were to flee evil (Matt. 10.23).

This description of the life-style of the small group Jesus called to be with him has been applied by the evangelists to the life of all Christians. Yet this life-style does not fit, as far as we can tell, that of the early leaders of the Christian Church, let alone that followed by Christians down the ages. After the crucifixion at least some of the disciples returned to their homes and their trades in Galilee (Matt. 28.16, Jn. 21). We soon find Christian communities organized throughout the empire, meeting for worship in private homes. When Paul visited Jerusalem three years after his conversion he found Peter in residence (Gal. 1.18). Fifteen years later on a visit he found the "three pillars" of the Church, James, Peter and John, in residence. Most Christians, even in those early days, seem to have lived a settled life and to have had a "home." Nor did those early leaders of the Church reject the family even though we are told that Jesus said "If any one comes to me and does not hate his own father and mother and wife and children and brothers and sisters, yes, and even his own life, he cannot be my disciple" (Lk. 14.26). Paul tells the Corinthians that he has no command of the Lord on the subject but his opinion is "Are you bound to a wife? Do not seek to be free. Are you free from a wife? Do not seek marriage." (1 Cor. 7.25f). He points out that he has the right "to be accompanied by a wife as the other apostles and brothers of the Lord and Cephas" (1 Cor. 9.5). There is no thought that these leaders should "have made themselves eunuchs for the sake of the kingdom of heaven" (Matt. 19.12). Nor is there any thought that these leaders should follow the words of Jesus and "not be anxious about your life, what you shall eat or what you shall drink nor about your body, what you shall put on" (Matt. 6.25). Paul tells the Corinthians that, with Barnabas, he has a rightful claim on them for support (1 Cor. 9.3f), and he tells us that "the Lord commanded that those who proclaim the gospel should get their living by the gospel" (1 Cor. 9.14). Some of his energy was spent in organizing a collection for the poor of Jerusalem (Rom. 15.25f, 1 Cor. 16.1–4). Nor do we find that the early Christians rejected all rights and protection. The disciple we know most about was not one to turn the other cheek. He lived his life in the midst of conflict. He called his opponents "false apostles, deceitful workmen," comparing them with Satan himself (2 Cor. 11.13, 14). He alludes to them as "the dogs" (Phil. 3.2) and wishes that those who preached circumcision to the gentiles would castrate themselves. (Gal. 5.12). He seemed to enjoy the law court and probably was sent to Rome on a legal appeal (Acts 25.12). It would seem that the gospel teaching about discipleship refers primarily to the group organized by Jesus.

In recent years the study of small groups has been one of the major areas of research in sociology and social psychology. The "group" has been shown to be very effective in therapy and sensitivity training. It is used in the treatment of alcoholics. It is used in communist cells. The small group has been found, according to C.R. Shepherd in his book *Small Groups*,[74] to be "an essential mechanism of socialization and the primary source of social order. There is little doubt that a small group provides the major source of the values and attitudes people have, and an important source of pressures to conform to social values and attitudes." Shepherd goes on to list the generally accepted criteria for a small group. (1) A small group is more organized and enduring than a group that would meet for some special purpose but not as organized or enduring as a formal organization. (2) Such a group would have more than two or three members and probably not more than fifteen. (3) Most members of the group would share a similar background and probably come from the same area. (4) The group would have common objectives and shared values.

The group about Jesus, the twelve, meets all these criteria. Such a group we are told is more organized and enduring than a group that would meet only for some special purpose, such as those who would gather to hear Jesus preach, yet not as organized and enduring as a formal organization. In Mark's gospel the call of the first disciples seems to be almost casual. It is almost as though Jesus just happened to be passing the lakeshore when he said to the fisherman, "Follow me and I will make you become fishers of men" (Mk. 1.17). The four fishermen continue in the company of Jesus. There is a subsequent call to Levi to leave his toll station, (Mk. 2.14f) and then the appointment of the twelve, "to be with him" (Mk. 3.14).

There are four lists of the names of the twelve in the New Testament (Matt. 10.2f, Mk. 3.16f, Lk. 6.14f, Acts 1.13f). John refers to the twelve in 6.67f and mentions Thomas as belonging to the group in 20.24. The lists in Matthew and Mark agree except in order, as do those in Luke and Acts. The last two lists differ from the first two in having "Judas the son of James" instead of Thaddaeus. The twelve appear in the gospels as the constant companions of Jesus and as those to whom Jesus' teaching was specially addressed (e.g., Mk. 9.35, 10.32). Matthew and Luke refer to them as the twelve disciples (e.g., Matt. 10.1, Lk. 9.1) or the twelve apostles (Matt. 10.2, Lk. 22.14). This confusion over the names has led some to suggest that the sayings that mention the twelve do not go back to Jesus.[75] Sanders rejects these suggestions arguing that Paul accepted that there was a special group called the twelve (1 Cor. 15.5), that the betrayal by one of them, Judas, could hardly have been invented, and that the disagreement over the names counts for rather than against the existence of a group of twelve about Jesus.[76] Some have suggested, however, that the appointment of the twelve meant the formation of that formal and enduring organization which we call the Christian Church. There are texts supporting this position, but most texts that support the granting of powers to the apostles for the life of the Church, for example Matthew 16.17–19, 18.18, 28.18–20, Luke 24.46–49, John 20.23, 21.15–23, seem to be the product of the early Church's quest for authority. Certainly the twelve are prominent at the resurrection and at the election of Matthias (Acts 1.15f). Yet in Acts we see the leadership in Jerusalem soon passing from the original apostles to other groups in which James, the Lord's brother, took a leading part. There is no mention in the writings of Paul of the twelve continuing as a group and governing the Church. When Paul first visited Jerusalem three years after his conversion, Peter was the only member of the twelve mentioned (Gal. 1.18). Fifteen years later he met those in authority in Jerusalem, the "pillars" of the Church, and they were James, Cephas and John (Gal. 2.9). We know that Peter himself was often travelling about (Acts 8.14, 9.32f, Gal. 2.11, 1 Cor. 1.12), and it seems that the group of twelve under his leadership soon disappeared.

The twelve men that Jesus "appointed to be with him" (Mk. 3.14), therefore, meet the first criterion for a small group. "The twelve" were organized and enduring in that they lasted as a group for the whole of Christ's ministry, including the resurrection appearances, yet as a group they never became a formal organization even though there were those in the early Church who felt they should have become a formal enduring organization.

Another criterion for a small group is that it have more than two or three members but probably not more than fifteen. The number appointed by Jesus meets this criterion. We should, however, stress the word "appointed." So often we think of Jesus gathering followers or disciples as he went along. However, the relationship that "the twelve" had with Jesus was not that of a student-master relationship initiated by the pupil. In the synoptic gospels Jesus finds these men and appoints them to their position. It is only in John that we find the story told the other way about. He tells us that two disciples of John the Baptist leave John and follow Jesus. They in turn recruit others with the words, "We have found him of whom Moses in the law and also the prophets did write, Jesus of Nazareth, the son of Joseph" (Jn. 1.45). In Mark's gospel Jesus has only just begun preaching the "gospel of God" when he comes upon Simon Peter and Andrew and tells them "follow me." It is not a request, it is a command. They are not asked to follow in a literal sense, they are ordered to be disciples. We then have a similar scene with James and John. Later Jesus finds Levi, sitting at a tax office and says to him "follow me." In the subsequent appointment of the twelve, Jesus separates himself from the multitude and going apart on a hill he calls those he wants "and they came to him." He then appoints the twelve to their task (Mk. 3.13f).[77] As a sign of the new age Jesus may have given some of the disciples a new name. Perhaps the confusion over the names of the twelve is a result of this. Peter was remembered because of the play upon *Petros*—the rock, but Boanerges (Mk. 3.17) could be a combination of names.

The twelve were to be foundation stones, the nucleus, of the holy eschatological community of the kingdom of God. They were to sit on twelve thrones judging the twelve tribes of Israel (Matt. 19.28). They were sent out "with authority" (Mk. 3.15, 6.7). They were given the "keys of the kingdom" (Matt. 16.19). After they returned from their mission their presence is mentioned on all important occasions on the way up to Jerusalem (Mk. 10.32) and at the "last supper" (Mk. 14.17). Peter, James and John are present at the raising of the daughter of Jairus

(Mk. 5.37), the transfiguration (Mk. 9.2), and Gethsemane (Mk. 14.33). The group of twelve, formed and trained by Jesus, continued with him in his earthly ministry.

Another criterion for a small group is that "most members would share a similar background and come from a similar area." We do not know the background of all of "the twelve" but we do know that the first few to be called were fishermen (Mk. 1.16f, par., Jn. 21f). There are a number of indications that Capernaum was a kind of home to Jesus. In John 6.16, after Jesus leaves the disciples, they set out to go home, crossing the sea to Capernaum. John 2.12 tells us that Jesus went there with his mother, his brothers and disciples suggesting a family connection with the town. This passage can more naturally be translated "and there *he* stayed for a few days," which implies that his family and disciples lived there. In Matthew 4.13 we are told that Jesus left Nazareth and "went and dwelt in Capernaum." In Mark 2.1, after Jesus has returned to Capernaum, it was "reported that he was at home."

In the synoptics much of the teaching addressed to the disciples by Jesus takes place "when he had entered the house and left the people (and) his disciples asked him" (Mk. 7.17). In Mark, "the house" is the setting for nineteen pericopes. He specifically mentions the house as the scene of the activity of Jesus on eleven occasions (Mk. 1.29, 2.1, 15, 3.19bf, 5.38, 7.17, 24, 9.28, 33, 10.10. 14.3). Matthew and Luke change many of these settings, for instance Mark begins the passage on humility with these words "and they came to Capernaum; and when he was in the house he asked them" (Mk. 9.33). Matthew and Luke omit this passage. In Luke the discussion is in private with the disciples but there is no mention of them entering a house (Lk. 9.43b–45). In Matthew the setting is provided by verse 22 of Chapter 17. The preferred reading should probably be "and while they abode in Galilee" rather than the "as they were gathering" accepted by the R.S.V. On two occasions Matthew makes use of the house as a setting for the teaching of Jesus independently of Mark or "Q" (Matt. 9.28, 13.36). G. Strecker argues that the way Matthew uses the word "house" shows that he had a specific house in mind, a dwelling in Capernaum that was home to Jesus and the disciples.[78]

The synoptics suggest that Capernaum was the home of Peter and Andrew, whereas John tells us that they were from Bethsaida. Bethsaida was a short walk from Capernaum and it was perhaps where they kept their boats. The tradition then that we find in the gospels is that in

the early days of his ministry Jesus had close ties with the small and
often anonymous communities near the lake but a special tie with
Capernaum. People noticed that his disciples spoke with a Galilean ac-
cent. When Hellenistic cities are mentioned, Jesus enters only the surrounding countryside. He touches on the "villages of Caesarea Phil-
lipi" (Mk. 8.27), the "region of Tyre" and the "country of the
Gerasenes" (Mk. 5.1). There was a Church at Tyre in the early days
(Acts 21.3f) and if Jesus had entered the city it would have been remembered. The larger towns of Galilee, the capital Sepphoris, four miles
from Nazareth, Tarichaeae, Gamala, and other places go unmentioned
in the gospels. Despite the tradition that Jesus was a carpenter's son
(Matt. 13.55) we hear little about craftsmen and merchants and a great
deal about farmers, fishermen, vintners and shepherds. Jerusalem was
the only city and even it was avoided at night as Jesus would retreat to
Bethany. It was a place that kept killing the prophets (Lk. 13.33f), its
temple had become a den of robbers (Mk. 11.15f). The gospels would
lead us to believe that the men appointed by Jesus to this small group
were country bred and from a small area near the sea of Galilee.[79]

The final mark of a small group is that it "would have common objectives and shared values." More accurately, perhaps, the group would
come to have common objectives and shared values. The group about
Jesus emerged at a time of social crisis in Palestinian Judaism. It was a
time that brought forward many renewal movements. Most godly
people looked for the restoration of Israel. It was promised in scripture.
It was an important part of the Jewish literature of the time. Jesus and
his followers lived within the framework of those eschatological expectations. He did not focus on the means of bringing the kingdom, as
far as we can tell he did not look for a military or political solution. Yet
he was certain that God would soon restore Israel.[80] This was something
many people wanted to believe. The twelve came to share that vision, a
vision that included the restoration of the temple (Mk. 14.57f, Matt.
26.60f), the ingathering of the twelve tribes (Micah 2.12, Isa. 11.11f,
Matt. 10.6) and, we would suggest, the salvation of the gentiles.

There were many people who shared this vision. Through all the gospels it is often difficult to determine whether "his disciples" means a
small group living in close fellowship with Jesus or a larger body of
those who have accepted him as their leader or teacher. Matthew and
Mark seem to refer regularly to a small group, small enough to gather in
a house (Mk. 9.28) or in a boat (Mk. 6.45). Luke, however, tends to

speak of a great "crowd of his disciples" (Lk. 6.17, 19.37). John also speak of many disciples and tells of those who desert after a prediction of the passion (Jn. 6.59f). The openness of Jesus toward women is reported in all the gospels but particularly in Luke. Among this larger group of disciples there were many women. Luke connects three women with the twelve. The Martha and Mary story tells of their care for Jesus in their home (Lk. 10.38f). Other women were among the "great multitude" that followed Jesus to Golgotha (Lk. 23.27f). Some of these would have been "the women who came with him from Galilee" (Lk. 23.55). Another party that came to Jerusalem were his "brethren," Mary his mother with his brothers and sisters (Jn. 2.12, 7.3, Matt. 12.46, 13.55). They had refused to accept his claims and, according to Mk. 3.21, they had thought him to be out of his mind, although as a group they became important after the resurrection.

Among the many people who were influenced by Jesus, there was a special group of men who lived with him called the twelve. With this group Jesus lived his life of prayer, with them he shared the signs of the kingdom, the healing of the sick, the casting out of demons. He taught them of God's judgement, of his forgiveness. It was this small group, the primary group of Christianity, that, with the women who followed from Galilee, came to be the first witnesses of the resurrection.

The experience to be found in a small group has been summarized in these words, "The essential emotional bond that participants have for the group seems to derive from categories of experience other than learning and practicing specific interpersonal skills. These are related to the internal substance and dynamics of the group and include:

– experiencing a rare sense of community;

– becoming close to people in an unusually intense way;

– being able to share their warmth with another person, particularly of the same sex and especially between men;

– becoming free to reveal themselves as people;

– developing a sense of their own personal worth that might have been previously lacking.

For reasons that are not altogether clear, human relations training groups, of whatever specific orientation, develop a culture that most participants find exhilarating. A positive group experience leaves people with a sense that they have not really been alive before, that they have experienced too little of the richness around them."[81] The small group that Jesus appointed "to be with him" must have shared something of these emotions.

2. Cross-Bearing

One of the marks of discipleship that separated the small group that lived with Jesus from the greater number of followers was the demand that he made of the twelve that they bear their own cross. There are a number of sayings that make this clear. In Mark 8.34 we read that Jesus called "the multitude with the disciples" after Peter had rebuked him for speaking of the suffering he faced, "and he said to them if any man would come after me, let him deny himself and take up his cross and follow me." Matthew has the same passage except he clears up the ambiguity by making the passage apply only to his close disciples (Matt. 16.24). In Luke it is clear from the context that it applies only to his close disciples. Some manuscripts of Luke 9.23 speak about taking up the cross "daily." This addition may be seen as an attempt to spiritualize the saying and make it apply to all Christians. In the same way other more general statements about losing one's life in order to save one's life are often inserted into the context of the Cross sayings. There is another set of sayings from "Q." Matthew has "and he who does not take up his cross and follow me is not worthy of me" (Matt. 10.38), whereas Luke has "Whoever does not bear his own cross and come after me cannot be my disciple" (Lk. 14.27).

The tendency of all gospel writers is to make the sayings of Jesus apply to their own time, to generalize and spiritualize his sayings. In an essay in the book *Suffering and Martyrdom in the New Testament,* J.C. O'Neill suggests that in these Cross sayings Jesus was both announcing his own willingness to be sacrificed and making it a condition of membership in his small, inner group of disciples.[82]

It is difficult to understand these passages in any other way. In their context these passages seem to imply that everyone would understand what taking up one's cross and following someone who was also carrying a cross would mean. It is usually suggested that the phrase "carrying one's cross" was a way of speaking about self-denial. After the crucifixion the phrase came to be used in that way. The solution, therefore, is to suggest that these passages are the work of the early Church. If we are prepared to agree that these passages are not authentic, then we have a possible explanation. The cross is often mentioned in the literature of the early Church but always with reference to the actual crucifixion of Jesus, yet the emphasis in these sayings is always on taking up and bearing one's own cross and following Jesus. O'Neill adds that "there is something ridiculous in the image of all Christians carrying crosses after Jesus, a ridiculousness we do not normally see because we spiritualize the language and covertly change the picture so that there is only one cross in view, the cross of Jesus."[83] On the other hand, if we suggest that the sayings are authentic and that they refer to the crucifixion, we are saying that Jesus called his disciples to go with him in his grim march toward a Roman crucifixion. Therefore, he was calling them to rebellion against Rome. This does not seem to be consistent with the other teaching of Jesus. It also seems a strange suggestion because a Roman criminal condemned to crucifixion had no choice as to whether he would or would not "carry his cross."

Vincent Taylor, in his commentary on St. Mark accepts the verse as authentic and suggests that it be read as a metaphor. He agrees that "It is by no means necessary to suppose that the metaphor is 'Christian' in the sense that the crucifixion of Christ is implied." He also agrees that such a catch phrase for self denial is not found in the older rabbinic literature. He is therefore driven to suggest that "death by crucifixion under the Romans was a sufficiently familiar sight in Palestine to be the basis of the saying." This would mean that Jesus was asking his followers to court Roman execution and to follow him as he marched toward his own execution. As O'Neill suggests, we are faced with a dilemma. If the sayings have a "religious" meaning we are forced to conclude that they are inauthentic, because they were attributed to Jesus by the early Church and refer to disciples following Jesus to crucifixion just as Jesus faced his crucifixion. Alternatively, however, we must conclude, as Vincent Taylor does, that the sayings have a straightforward political meaning, a call to defy Rome, in which case they betray an attitude untypical of the generally pacific tenor of the teaching of Jesus.[84]

It is the details of these sayings, their emphasis on voluntarily taking and bearing the cross and following Jesus, rather than on the actual crucifixion of Jesus, that brings us to look for another interpretation.

There is rabbinic evidence that the verse in Genesis 22.6 that says: "and Abraham took the wood of the burnt offering and laid it upon Isaac his son" was interpreted to mean "as he who carries his cross on his shoulders."[85] If this rabbinic teaching was well known, we can understand why the Cross saying seems to imply that everyone knew what Jesus meant by taking up one's cross and following him as he carried his own cross.[86] According to Jewish teaching, Isaac was an exemplary martyr, and it is possible that he was seen as more than just an example of religious devotion. It is possible to suggest that the offering of Isaac was seen as an expiatory and redemptive act for all Israel. In the fourth book of Maccabees there are references to such expiatory martyrdom and all but one of the references to Isaac in the book occur in the account of the martyrdom of the seven brothers and their mother in Chapters 8 to 18. In these passages Isaac's self-offering is not only an example, but also a sacrifice and a burnt-offering, for this is what the mother calls her sons to in Chapter 16.19f and 18.88. It is said that the offering of the seven brothers and their mother was to purify their country, to be a ransom for the nation's sins, to be blood shed as propitiation, and to lead to the salvation of Israel (4 Macc. 17.22, cf., 18. 3–5).

Matthew 10.38 speaks of one who takes up his cross and follows as being "worthy" of Jesus. O'Neill points out that this helps confirm his interpretation.[87] It is no vague sentiment. The last of the seven brothers to be put to death is exhorted by his mother to be "worthy" (2 Macc. 7.29). The martyrs in Revelation are said to be "worthy" (Rev. 3.4, 16.6). In Wisdom, the "souls of the righteous" are found "worthy" (Wis. 3.5).

Thus it appears that in the Cross sayings Jesus announced his own willingness to be sacrificed for the people's sins and made it a condition of the call to discipleship that they should be willing, like Isaac, to take the wood of the cross on their own shoulders. This means that these sayings were not meant to apply to all who believe in Jesus. They are restricted to the small group who are prepared to bear the sins of those who have broken God's law, those who deserve God's punishment. We are told that the last of the seven brothers prayed that his death with that of his brothers would "end the wrath of the Almighty which has justly fallen on our whole nation" (2 Macc. 7.38). This saying about following the cross was soon spiritualized by the early Church so that it applied to all Christians. Some manuscripts of Luke 9.23 talk about taking

up the cross "daily" and, as we have seen, Mark 8.34 makes the saying
apply to the crowd as well as the disciples. All the gospels connect the
saying with the one that speaks of losing one's life in order to save one's
life. Jesus could never have suggested that all Israel be martyrs. We are
forced therefore to see the original saying as intended by Jesus to apply
to his immediate disciples. The possibility of martyrdom was a condition of membership in the small group.

We should consider another saying of Jesus that mentions the possible death of his followers. This is the saying "Truly, I say to you,
there are some standing here who will not taste death before the kingdom of God is come with power" (Mk. 9.1, par.). J. C. O'Neill
points out that as the saying stands it is rather banal.[88] If we knew the age
of the youngest present, using the expected life span of that time we
could calculate when Jesus expected the kingdom to come. The saying
must have meant more than this. The death of some of the disciples
seems to be connected in some way with the coming of the kingdom.
The solution proposed is that a corruption has crept into the text. Jesus
originally spoke not of those standing "here" but simply of those standing. There is textual evidence, which O'Neill sets out, that would support this suggestion.[89] In all three texts the position of the word "here"
is uncertain. In each case there is some evidence that the word was not
found. Without the word "here" we have what would be called a
"hard" reading. It is a reading that would attract the addition of
"here." The solution suggested is that we accept the shorter text and
understand "those who stand" to mean those who withstand persecution. The word "to stand" is used in the New Testament to mean "to
face persecution" (Eph. 6.11, 13, 14, Rev. 6.17). The same verb is
used to mean withstanding God's judgement in Psalm 130.3.

The Seer asks in Revelation 6.17, "For the great day of their wrath
has come and who can stand before it?" Our saying is to be understood
as a reply to such a question. Jesus is prophesying and saying "There
are some who withstand who will not taste death before the kingdom of
God is come with power." This would imply that Jesus expected to die
with some of his small group, but if they all stood firm, some of them
need not die as martyrs before the kingdom comes.

As soon as we accept the suggestion that these sayings of Jesus refer
to the sacrifice of Isaac, we can understand the emphasis in the sayings
on voluntarily taking up and bearing one's cross to follow Jesus. As we
have seen, this is where the emphasis in the sayings lies, not on actual
crucifixion. The term "the cross" can be seen as quite appropriate to

the story of Isaac. The wooden cross could easily have been spoken of as the wood of sacrifice before the time of Jesus. Jews had already been crucified for their faith and the ambiguity of "wood" and "tree" had already been used to connect the tree in the garden of Eden with the staff on which the brazen serpent had been lifted up in the wilderness.[90] Martyrs' deaths before the time of Jesus had been seen as atoning for the sins of the people and the rabbinic interpretation of the wood for sacrifice as a cross, cited above, shows the further connection.[91]

O'Neill thinks that the best support for his view that Jesus specifically prepared a few to suffer for many is that "these few are those who were called to rule over many."[92] He points out that every saying about service in the synoptic gospels, where we can determine the scope of the audience, is directed solely to the inner group. Jesus contrasts the way the small group will rule as servants of all with the way the gentiles rule (Mk. 10.42–44 & par.) as they sit judging the twelve tribes of Israel (Matt. 19.28). Perhaps O'Neill presses the argument too far when he suggests that Jesus looked toward his own death and the death of the disciples as a sacrifice for sin. Yet we can trace the Cross sayings back to the wood of sacrifice and the story of Abraham and Isaac. When the twelve answered the demand of Jesus that they bear their own cross, they knew that they faced the possibility of martyrdom.[93]

This suggestion supports those who argue that, at the time of Jesus, there was a widespread expectation that a messianic prophet would be sent by God and that this prophet would be martyred and then vindicated by God. F. Schussler-Fiorenza tells us in his *Foundational Theology* that Mark 6.14 ("Some said, John the Baptizer has been raised from the dead") is evidence that "The Jewish tradition of martyrdom and resurrection of eschatological figures (Elijah and Enoch) had in Jesus' lifetime been applied to the fate of John the Baptizer."[94] He believes that this approach to understanding the preparation of the disciples by Jesus, particularly as set out in the teaching of Pesch and Schillebeeckx, has many advantages. He does admit, however, that many of their assumptions have been challenged and much of the data possibly comes from a period later than that of the New Testament.

If we agree that Jesus looked to a martyrdom with his disciples we must then suppose that he also spoke of his victory and resurrection. We cannot begin a study of the messianic consciousness of Jesus or of the use of "Son of Man," but we can suggest that Jesus denied the finality of evil.[95] In John's gospel the raising of Lazarus (Ch. 11), which dramatizes the teaching of Jesus on resurrection is placed at the beginning of the passion narrative. The synoptics all record three predictions of the passion (Mk. 8.31, 9.31, 10.33f, par.). These predictions, mentioning "after three days," are too detailed for Bultmann. He asks "can there be any doubt that they are all *vaticinia ex eventu*?"[96] He goes on to argue that the idea of a dying and rising Messiah or Son of Man was unknown in Judaism and therefore these passages must be the work of the early Church. On the other hand, Hans Bayer, after a thorough study of all the evidence concludes that these three predictions are the "primary evidence in support of the possibility that Jesus did indeed speak of his death and resurrection."[97] Our suggestion is that as Jesus expected the parousia, he used the biblical expression "after three days" to mean "in a short time" (Gen. 42.17, Hos. 6.2) when he spoke to the disciples about what was to happen in the future. John has probably preserved this tradition of Jesus' discussion with his disciples in the various passages in which he has Jesus speak of what will come about in "a little while" (Jn. 14.19, 16.16–24 and related sayings such as Jn. 7.33, 34, 8.21, 12.35, 13.33). Mark, faithful to the tradition he has received, uses the expression "after three days," whereas it is changed by Matthew and Luke to read "on the third day." After the event they felt that they should sharpen the reference to the resurrection.

Just after the third prediction of the passion, Jesus asks two of his disciples "Are you able to drink the cup that I drink, or be baptized with the baptism with which I am baptized?" (Mk. 10.38). Matthew repeats the saying about the cup (Matt. 20.22) while Luke repeats the saying about baptism (Lk. 12.50). In the Old Testament the cup is often a symbol of suffering (Isa. 51.17, 22, Jer. 25.15, Ezek. 23.32, Lam. 4.21, Ps. 75.8). The book that tells of "The Martyrdom of Isaiah" speaks of the "cup of martyrdom" (Mart. of Isa. 5.13). The figure of baptism again often expresses the idea of suffering or of being overwhelmed or going under (Ps. 42.7, 69.2, 15, Isa. 43.2, Isa. 21.4 LXX has "unrighteousness baptizes me"). This pericope ends with a passage we should consider. We are told that the life of the Son of Man is to be given as "a ransom for many" (Mk. 10.45, Matt. 20.28). This passage can be understood as referring to the benefits to come from the death of a martyr.[98] The Old Testament background of the saying is in the Servant Songs of Isaiah, perhaps especially verse 43.3 that speaks of Egypt being given as a ransom.

The point of the rather difficult passage that Mark records, "For everyone will be salted with fire" (Mk. 9.49), is that the disciples must be ready to face the fire of sacrifice. In the Old Testament salt is often connected with sacrifice (Lev. 2.13, Num. 18.19, Ezek 43.24). The "salt of the covenant" is to be offered in the fire of sacrifice. Mark connects this saying with the saying that tells of salt losing its saltness (Mk. 9.49, 50, Matt. 5.13, Lk. 14.34). Matthew has his version of the saying about salt (best translated as in the N.E.B.) "You are salt to the world" (Matt. 5.13) follow a passage that tells the disciples to rejoice in persecution because "so persecuted the prophets who were before you" (Matt. 5.12).

Jesus looked beyond death to the perfect fellowship of the consummated kingdom. He told his disciples at their last supper together that he would not drink with them again until he would "drink it new with you in my Father's kingdom" (Matt. 26.29, par.). A "sign" of that consummated kingdom would be health, wholeness and holiness.

3. Healing and Exorcism

Jesus and the small group he gathered about him, shared a longing for a world renewed by God. The disciples were attracted to this man because they saw him as a rabbi, a prophet, an exorcist. Some, like Cleopas, saw Jesus as "a prophet mighty in deed and word before God and all the people" (Lk. 24.19). They looked for the restoration of Israel, they looked for a miraculous change in the historical situation, a cosmic catastrophe of apocalyptic intensity.

The healing ministry of Jesus must be seen against the background of these expectations. It is a mistake to see the healing ministry as simply an expression of the pastoral care of Jesus. Morton T. Kelsey, in his book *Healing and Christianity* put that position in these words: "The healing ministry of Jesus is certainly in line with the constant emphasis in his teachings on compassion and caring about one's neighbor... This stress on the importance of *agape,* love, is the most basic aspect of his teaching. One of the most concrete ways of expressing love is through concern about another's physical and emotional condition and the removal of torturing infirmities, physical hindrances and mental and emotional illness."[99]

On the other hand it is also a mistake to see the miracles of healing as explaining the divinity of Jesus or as a ratification of his claim to supernatural status. This traditional position was rejected by some of the form critics who tended to explain away the miracles. They saw them as tales or legends used to make a very human Jesus into a God in the same way

Hellenistic miracle tales were used to deify heroes. If we see the healing ministry of Jesus simply as an expression of love, it is difficult to understand why he did not organize a full scale "healing center." Why would he tell those healed not to tell others (Mk. 1.44)? Why would he take a boat to escape from the great crush of those who came to be healed (Mk. 3.9)? Yet, healing was too much a part of his ministry and the healings too diverse to be explained away as invented legends.

The picture that is given in the gospels is that of a "royal progress." It is as if a claimant to a medieval throne on a long journey to his coronation began to heal people with his "royal touch." People would see such miracles as a sign of God's pleasure and blessing on the claimant. So the gospels show the healing miracles as the "signs and wonders" and the "mighty works" of the royal progress of Jesus to his crucifixion-coronation in Jerusalem.

In Luke's account of the beginnings of his ministry, Jesus attends the synagogue on the Sabbath. He is given the book of Isaiah to read: "The Spirit of the Lord is upon me because he has anointed me to preach good news to the poor. He has sent me to proclaim release to the captives, the recovery of sight to the blind, to set at liberty those who are oppressed, to proclaim the acceptable year of the Lord" (Lk. 4.18). After resuming his seat he tells the assembly, "Today these words are fulfilled in your hearing" (Lk. 4.21). The healing ministry is seen as part of the proclamation of the "year of the Lord." In the "Q" collection we have the story of Jesus' reply to the disciples of John the Baptist, "Go and tell John what you have seen and heard, the blind receive their sight, the lame walk, lepers are cleansed and the deaf hear, the dead are raised up and the poor have the good news preached to them" (Lk. 7.22, 23).

A study of the way "the blind receive their sight" will show how the gospel writers understood the significance of this healing miracle. Accepting the shorter ending for Mark, each section of his Gospel ends with a reference to seeing. The first part of the gospel, which tells of Jesus' public ministry, ends at 8.22f with the healing of the blind man. The second part, which emphasizes the relationship between Jesus and his disciples, also ends with the healing of Bartimaeus, a blind beggar (Mk. 10.46f). Then Mark ends the passion narrative with the promise, "He is going on before you into Galilee, there you will see him" (Mk. 16.7). Mark's placing of these stories and the way he tells them seems to have special significance. The progressive character of the healing in Mark 8.22f can be seen as the evangelist's commentary on the gradual opening of the eyes of the disciples. So the second healing of a blind man may be seen as a commentary on the opening of the eyes of Peter. We see this same concern to show the healing miracles as the fulfillment of the Old Testament prophecy in the way Matthew places side by side his stories of the healing of the two blind men and the dumb demonic (Matt. 9.27f). The deaf hear, the dumb speak and the blind receive their sight. Of the seven miracles in John's gospel, the passage that tells the story of the man born blind begins with Jesus saying "I am the light of the world" (Jn. 8.12). Again we have the same emphasis on the opening of the eyes of the disciples. As in the other gospels, these miracles are signs, signs that open the eyes of all who believe in God's purpose for their time.

The Old Testament background for the healing ministry is apparent from the way in which the gospel writers present it as the fulfillment of Isaiah's promises and show how the eyes of the disciples were gradually opened to that fulfillment. It is apocalyptic literature that provides the background for the many references to exorcism. The power of Jesus over demons is seen in the New Testament as a special authentication of his divine mission. We see this attitude expressed at the beginning of Mark's gospel, "What is this? A new kind of teaching? With authority he commands even unclean spirits, and they obey him" (Mk. 1.27). In the Johannine tradition a similar idea is expressed in 1 John 3.8, "The reason the Son of God appeared was to destroy the works of the devil." The importance of exorcism in the ministry of Jesus is shown by Mark's report that in his lifetime Jewish exorcists were using his name to cast out demons (Mk. 9.38). In a world that accepted the idea that much of life was controlled by demons, exorcism was of great importance. The Pauline tradition sums up the prevailing attitude in Ephesians 6.12f: "For we are not contending against flesh and blood, but against the principalities, against powers, against the world rulers of this present darkness, against the spiritual hosts of wickedness in the heavenly places." Demons were thought to inhabit people or animals unpredictably, and without known reason. They must have a body in which to reside (Matt. 12.45, Mk. 5.1f). It is the demons themselves that recognize the power of Jesus (Mk. 1.34, James 2.19). Even the demons had their part to play in the proclamation of the message of Jesus. This is the point of the Beelzebub controversy recorded by both Mark (3.22f) and "Q" (Matt. 12.22f, and Lk. 11.14f). An accusation was made that Jesus cast out demons by the power of Beelzebub, the prince of demons. Jesus replies that the power of evil cannot be divided because a kingdom so divided would fall. In the "Q" version Jesus returns the accusation by suggesting that if he had exorcised demons by Beelzebub perhaps the same was true of Pharisaic exorcists. He then goes on to say "But if I by the finger of God (Matt. 12.28: Spirit of God) cast out demons, then the kingdom of God is come upon you" (Lk. 11.20). In all three gospels this passage is followed by the parable of the strong man's house. The point made is that the strong man has been bound by a stronger power, his house is being despoiled, the mighty works of Jesus are the miracles that point to a new age.

Jesus saw these "signs" as inseparable from his person and his work. They are not a proof of divinity, indeed even false messiahs and false prophets show "signs and wonders" (Mk. 13.22, par.). In these signs the "reality" of the future appears, not just an omen of the future. They are anticipations of the imminent kingdom of God. Just as the kingdom does not come by calculation or observation, for "you do not know when the time will come" (Mk. 13.33, par.), so neither can these miracles offer proof that Jesus is the Messiah. This is the point of the passage about Beelzebub and the sons of the Pharisees (Matt. 12.22–30, par.). People are blind to the true signs of the time, they can tell weather signs but they cannot tell the signs of the present (Lk. 12.54–56, Mk. 13.28f).

Demands were made that Jesus prove who he was by a sign but he seems to have rejected these demands more than once. His mighty acts were acts of God but those who demanded signs could not read "the signs of the times" (Matt. 16.3, Lk. 12.54–56). After the feeding of the four thousand the Pharisees seek a sign from heaven (Mk. 8.11–13, par.). In a "Q" passage those who demand a sign are told that the only sign they will have is "the sign of Jonah" (Matt. 12.38-40, Lk. 11.29, 30), the sign of a preacher of repentance. The high priests and the scribes even demand a sign of power when he is on the cross (Mk. 15.32, par.). There was a tradition that a prophet had to authenticate himself by a sign.[100] This demand for a sign is set out clearly in John's gospel (e.g., Jn. 2.23, 6.30). Jesus refuses to perform this kind of a sign (e.g., Jn. 4.48). In his miracles, Jesus performs the "works of God" (Jn. 9.3). His disciples see the work he is doing (Jn. 7.3) and are to share in this work which is to "believe in him whom he has sent" (Jn. 6.29). As the disciples come to believe even "for the sake of the works themselves" (Jn. 14.11), they are promised that "Truly, truly, I say to you, he who believes in me will do the works that I do; and greater works than these will he do" (Jn. 14.12). Others who have also seen these works of Jesus reject them in blindness and disobedience (e.g.,

Jn. 9.29–41, 12.37) or did not confess them for fear of the Pharisees (Jn. 12.42f). These works of Jesus interpret one another but together they witness to the revelation of the glory of Jesus.[101] Yet "Jesus did many other signs in the presence of his disciples, which are not written in this book; but these are written that you might believe that Jesus is the Christ, the Son of God, and that believing you might have life in his name" (Jn. 20.30, 31).

When we come to look at the commission that Jesus gave to his disciples as he sent them out two by two, we find that they were sent to proclaim the kingdom. An important part of that proclamation was the casting out of demons and the healing of the sick. The directions given are reported four times in the gospels, each time the command to heal and to cast out demons is placed beside the command to preach. Mark summarizes the mission with the words "So they went out and preached that men should repent and they cast out many demons and anointed with oil many that were sick and healed them" (Mk. 6.12, 13). This summary may well reflect the teaching of the early Church. The commission to the disciples in Mark only mentions them going out to exorcize demons (Mk. 6.7). The commission in Matthew is quite extensive. Matthew seems to have had his own material to add to Mark and "Q's" versions. As in Luke, the original commission now consists of instructions to take "authority" over unclean spirits and to heal disease (Matt. 10.1). Luke has "He gave them power and authority over all devils and to cure diseases" (Lk. 9.1). Matthew adds the exhortation "And as you go, preach, saying, the kingdom of heaven is at hand, heal the sick, cleanse the lepers, cast out the devils, freely you received, freely give" (Matt. 10.7, 8). Luke tells us of two missions. The mission of "the twelve" follows quite closely the version in Mark with the addition of "and to cure disease" to the granting of authority over devils. The second version seems to follow the "Q" story more closely and tells of a mission of seventy others who are sent out two by two. These are sent, following the Lord's example, to heal the sick and to preach the kingdom of God. There is no mention of exorcism. It has long been thought that Luke intended the mission of the twelve to symbolize the mission to the twelve tribes of Israel and the mission to the seventy to symbolize the mission to the seventy nations of the gentiles.

We see something of the relationship between Jesus and the disciples in the healing ministry when we study Mark's story of the healing of the demon-possessed boy (Mk. 9.14–29). After "He began to teach them that the Son of Man must suffer many things ... and be killed and after

three days rise again" (Mk. 8.31) Peter, James and John go with Jesus
to a high mountain where Jesus is transfigured. As they return, they still
question "what rising from the dead meant?" (Mk. 9.10). They come
to the other disciples who are engaged in argument with the crowd. A
demon-possessed boy has been brought to them for healing, but they
have been unable to cast out the demon and the boy's father turns to
Jesus. There is almost the implication in the father's words that the
disciples' failure is a reflection on their master. Jesus replies by
commanding the spirit to depart. His comment "Oh faithless generation" (Mk. 9.19) seems to include the disciples for he later tells them
not to rely on their own powers but on the power of God (Mk. 9.29).
This passage shows us that the disciples were known to be trained
exorcists, indeed they were expected to be able to deal with even the
most difficult exorcism in the absence of Jesus. Afterward, in private,
they receive further instruction so that they will be able to deal with
such cases in the future.

Exorcism and healing were part of the training of the disciples. Although the reports of their work are probably influenced by what was
happening in the early Church when the gospels were written, it seems
certain that Jesus saw his healing ministry as a "sign of the kingdom"
and that he trained the twelve to share in that ministry.

4. Prayer

We ended the last chapter by pointing to a passage in which Jesus tells
the disciples not to rely on their own powers but on the power of God.
He tells the disciples "This kind (of demon) cannot be driven out by
anything but prayer" (Mk. 9.29). One of the marks of membership in
the small group that was formed by Jesus was the way he had them
share in his own special relationship with God through a life of prayer.
In his introduction to the Lord's Prayer, Luke has one of the disciples
say to Jesus, "Lord, teach us to pray as John taught his disciples" (Lk.
11.1). It is difficult to believe that the disciples, raised in Judaism, did
not know how to pray. Prayer would have been a discipline from early
youth and they were not asking for lessons in its practice. What was being suggested was that their group have a special pattern of prayers that
would be peculiar to them alone.

We know that at that time, as today, religious groups had their characteristic form and pattern of prayers. The "Shema" was recited morn-

ing and evening by the devout Jew (Deut. 6.7). By the time of Jesus, the Pharisaic party seems to have developed their own pattern of daily prayer connected with the times of temple sacrifice. This is the practice referred to in Acts 3.1, 10.3, and the Didache 8.3. The brotherhood at the Dead Sea had a "Manual of Discipline" and various patterns of daily prayer and worship. We may gather from Luke 11.1 that John the Baptist's disciples had their own form and pattern of prayers.

When this disciple came to Jesus then, he was apparently asking Jesus for just such a pattern of prayer so that their little group would be like other religious groups. He was asking for directions about where and when they should pray, what they should pray about, what particular pattern of prayer their group should follow. Jesus replies "When you pray, say:" (Lk. 11.2) then follows Luke's version of the "Lord's Prayer."

It is difficult to understand just what Jesus meant when he gave his disciples this prayer. Every part of the prayer, except the passage about "daily" bread, calls on God to bring the kingdom. The person who prays these passages is praying that God may be all in all. The recent scholarly discussion of the "Lord's Prayer" is outlined by J.A.T. Robinson in *Twelve More New Testament Studies*.[102] The word we usually translate "daily" seems to be peculiar to the Lord's Prayer. It is an unusual word. Origen and Jerome took the word to mean "the real or the essential bread." The word can also be translated, supported by passages such as Luke 14.15 and John 6.32, as meaning "the bread of the coming day." We could therefore paraphrase the prayer as: Father, we pray for the day when your name will be hallowed, the day when your kingdom has come, when your will will be done. We pray that you will give us the bread of the coming day, the essential bread. Then we will be forgiven as we now forgive. Do not let us fail in the trial, save us from the evil one.

If we see the prayer in this way it is more an attitude to life than a liturgical prayer. This is why we do not have any direction about when or how it is to be used. Luke links the prayer with two short parables. The one suggests that the disciples must be persistent in prayer, "Ask, and it will be given you; seek, and you will find" (Lk. 11.9). The other suggests that the heavenly Father will give just and good gifts (Lk. 11.11f). The disciples are to live a life of persistent prayer but Jesus did not demand that they follow a peculiar pattern of prayer such as was followed by other religious groups.

There are other passages that support this suggestion. Jesus frequently condemns the pattern of prayer and devotion developed by the Pharisees. He tells his disciples that they must not be like some Pharisees who contrive to be noticed at prayer (Matt. 6.5). Jesus called them hypocrites. Apparently Jesus did not take part in the three periods of prayer at the Temple when in Jerusalem. Perhaps he felt that this type of prayer came under his condemnation of "vain repetitions" (Matt. 6.7).

Jesus also rejects other rules about fasting and almsgiving. The setting for the "Lord's Prayer" in Matthew connects the prayer with other teachings of Jesus about the devotional life (Matt. 6.1–18). In these passages Jesus is seen to be critical of many who practiced almsgiving, prayer and fasting. In Luke 5.29 to the end of the chapter the attitude of Jesus is made clear. After a "great feast" at the house of Levi they said to him "The disciples of John fast often and offer prayers and so do the disciples of the Pharisees, but yours eat and drink" (Lk. 5.33). The mention of prayer is absent in the parallel passages in Mark and Matthew but Luke is probably correct (Matt. 9.9–17, Mk. 2.13–22). Prayer and fasting belong together (Mk. 9.29, Matt. 17.21, Lk. 2.37, 5.33). Jesus replies "Can you make wedding guests fast while the bridegroom is with them?" (Lk. 5.34). We then have three little parables, a pattern often used by Jesus. In them Jesus contrasts the situation in Judaism with the situation of Jesus and the disciples. The time for fasting and special prayers would come but not while Jesus was with the disciples. Their time, like a wedding must be an occasion for joy (Lk. 5.34, 35, par.). The old forms of prayer and fasting cannot be followed because that would be like putting a patch on an old garment (Lk. 5.36) or putting new wine in an old skin (Lk. 5.37–39). The next section (Lk. 6.1–5, par.) tells of the disciples eating grain on the Sabbath. The Pharisees point out that what they are doing is not lawful. Jesus replies, with a rather rabbinic argument, that as religious rules did not apply to David and his disciples so such rules cannot apply to Jesus and his disciples. The "Son of Man" is Lord of the Sabbath and of all the disciplines of the religious life.

Bultmann suggests that in the Judaism of the time faith in God the Creator had weakened. God had retreated into the distance as a transcendent heavenly King even though the official theology did not accept such an understanding. With Jesus, as he puts it "God again became a God at hand," a power here and now enfolding, limiting, commanding everyone. Bultmann points to the difference between the ornate emotional forms of address used in Jewish prayer and the stark simplicity of "Father." In the teaching of Jesus, "God is near; he hears and understands the requests which come thronging to him, as a father understands the requests of his own child (Matt. 7.7–11, par., cf., Lk. 11.5–8, 18.1–5)."[103]

E.P. Sanders, in his book *Paul and Palestinian Judaism* shows that many of the rabbis of this period "cultivated the consciousness of the presence of God in a thorough, effective and methodical way."[104] He rejects Bultmann on this point as being unfair to the rabbis. The Halakah, (Midrash that defines the norms of conduct), make every event of the day a stimulus for prayer. Sanders shows that many of the early rabbis seem to have exercised a good deal of freedom in praying even the "fixed" prayers. He points to passages that show that there was some feeling against praying in a fixed form in favor of spontaneity. He quotes with approval a passage from Heinemann that says that in their daily prayer life the rabbis addressed God "unhesitatingly in the Thou-style, and the relationship between Him and man is seen both as an intimate one of mutual love as between father and son, and as one of dependence and awe."[105]

There are many passages that mention Jesus at prayer but none of them fit the liturgical practice of the time.[106] There is no mention in the gospels of Jesus reciting the Shema with his disciples morning and evening or taking part in the daily prayers connected with the temple worship. We read of the prayers of Jesus at Gethsemane (Mk. 14.32–42, par.) and of the three meditations in Matthew 11.25f. There are three prayers of Jesus in John's gospel (Jn. 11.41f, 12.27f, 17.1f). The general references to prayer cannot be connected with the times of liturgical prayer. In Luke 6.12, Jesus spends all night at prayer. In Mark 1.35 we find Jesus at prayer before sunrise. Mark also tells us of Jesus rejoining the disciples after a night of prayer "about the fourth watch of the night" (Mk. 6.48). Luke has many references to prayer not found in the other gospels but they do not fit any special pattern.

Jeremias suggests that although we know very little about the place of daily prayer in the life of Jesus we can be certain that "the three hours of prayer in particular were so universally observed among the Jews of Jesus' time that we are justified in including them in the comment 'as his custom was,' which is made in Luke with reference to Jesus' attendance at Sabbath worship (Luke 4.16)."[107] He goes on to list support for this statement, yet none of the texts he cites actually supports his claim. A reference to Jesus at prayer "a great while before day" (Mk. 1.35) cannot be used to support his participation in the morning obligations, neither can a reference to Jesus all night at prayer (Lk. 6.12) be used to suggest that the evening prayer was extended until dawn. Support for the suggestion that Jesus took part in afternoon prayer is particularly weak. Jesus may well have been familiar with the words of the first benediction of the Tephilla but that does not mean that he used that prayer every afternoon.

Jeremias agrees that Jesus was not content with the three times a day liturgical prayer. He points to the passages that tell of Jesus spending the night at prayer (Mk. 1.35, 6.46, Lk. 6.12). He suggests that perhaps Luke added his many references to Jesus at prayer because there was an old tradition that Jesus often prayed outside the regular hours, particularly at night.[108]

The reason that the prayers of Jesus do not fit any special pattern, indeed the reason he refused to be like other religious groups and develop a special form of devotion, is that Jesus, like some of the rabbis referred to by Sanders, lived constantly in the presence of God. We see this best in a passage in Luke's gospel. In the parable of the judge and the widow (Lk. 18.1–8) he tells his disciples "always to pray and not to lose heart." This can be taken as an instruction to "pray always and not lose heart." In contrast the next parable (Lk. 18.9–14) tells of the hypocrisy of the Pharisees at prayer. Luke follows his version of the Lord's Prayer with the story of the importunate friend. The disciples are then told "Ask and it will be given you; seek, and you will find; knock, and it will be opened to you" (Lk. 11.9).

The life of prayer for Jesus was a constant, continuing conversation with God the Father. He allowed his disciples to see that this relationship was the supreme reality of his life. His authority came from the way God revealed himself to him, as a father to a son. At the beginning of his ministry, at his baptism, a voice came from heaven saying "Thou art my beloved Son, with thee I am well pleased" (Mk. 1.10). At Gethsemane he prays, "Abba, Father, all things are possible to thee" (Mk. 14.36). At the tomb of Lazarus Jesus prays "Father, I thank thee that thou hast heard me" (Jn. 11.41). In Jerusalem Jesus prays, "Father, glorify thy name." Then a voice came from heaven, "I have glorified it and I will glorify it again" (Jn. 12.28). Near the crucifixion Jesus prays "Father the hour has come, glorify thy Son that the Son may glorify thee" (Jn. 17.1). The text that most clearly tells us of the way Jesus shared this knowledge of God the Father with his disciples is a passage common to Matthew and Luke, "I thank thee, Father, Lord of heaven

and earth, that thou hast hidden these things from the wise and understanding and revealed them to babes; yea Father, for such was thy gracious will. All things have been delivered to me by my Father; and no
one knows the Son except the Father and no one knows the Father except the Son and any one to whom the Son chooses to reveal him"
(Matt. 11.25–27, Lk. 10.21, 22). Some of these texts may not give us
the actual words of Jesus but they must give us the memory the disciples
had of the teaching of Jesus. The experience that Jesus had had of God
as Father was something that he came to share with his small group. It
shone through Jesus so that those who came to know him came to know
the Father.

The gospels are clear that Jesus always distinguished between "my
Father" (Mk. 14.36, par., Matt. 11.27, par.) and "your Father" (Lk.
6.36, 12.30, 32) or "your heavenly Father" (Mk. 11.25, par., Matt.
23.9). Jesus does not include himself with his disciples in saying "our
Father." When he gives the Lord's Prayer he says "When you pray,
say ... " (Lk. 11.2, Matt. 6.9). The point is very clearly put in John's
gospel where Jesus says "My Father and your Father" (Jn. 20.17).

What is unique about the prayer life of Jesus and his disciples is the
way he taught them to share his special relationship with God. In his
preaching Jesus often taught about the nature of God in parables that
spoke of an earthly father (e.g., Lk. 15.11–32, Matt. 21.28f). When
Jesus came to speak of his own intimate and unique relationship with
God the Father he reserved those thoughts and feelings for the small
group he had chosen.

In his famous study, *The Prayers of Jesus*, Joachim Jeremias suggests that the most astonishing thing about the Lord's Prayer is that
"Jesus authorizes his disciples to repeat the word *Abba* after him. He
gives them a share in his sonship and empowers them, as his disciples,
to speak with their heavenly Father in just such a familiar, trusting way
as a child would with his father."[109] Jeremias connects the passage in
Matthew that says "unless you turn and become like children you will
never enter the kingdom of heaven" (Matt. 18.3) with this use of what
he calls a children's word for father. His argument is that, since the
Lord's Prayer represents a brief summary of the central elements of
Jesus' preaching, the giving of the prayer to the disciples authorized
them to say *Abba*, just as Jesus did. This allowed them to share in
Jesus' relationship with God.[110] Jeremias suggests that Jesus protected
this new form of address *Abba* in everyday speech. According to
Matthew 23.9, Jesus said "Call no man father on earth, for you have

one Father, who is in heaven." This prohibition against the disciples using an everyday courtesy title loses its strangeness if we see it as a protection of the address *Abba* from profanation.[111]

Both pagans and Jews used the word "Father" for God. In the Old Testament the Hebrew word *ab* is used, usually in a passage like "Oh Lord, thou art our Father" (Isa. 64.8). The image was also used in Jewish devotion. Yet the Jews were very hesitant about the use of this term for God. It is the way Jesus used the word *Abba*, the Aramaic word for father that is distinctive. Jesus spoke of God as Father in a way that suggested that it was a natural relationship. This intimate way of addressing God was remembered in the early Church. Paul wrote to the Galatians and the Romans using this Aramaic word and then translating it in addressing these Greek speaking communities (Gal. 4.6, Rom. 8.15). In the synoptic gospels Jesus only speaks of God as his Father when speaking to the disciples or while praying in the presence of his close disciples. The only exception is in the many references in Matthew's "Sermon on the Mount" and, as we shall see, the "sermon" can be understood as being addressed to the disciples alone. Only in John's gospel is the teaching not limited to the disciples. Here the emphasis on the communion between God the Father and Jesus becomes the central point of the message of Jesus to the "Jews."

Jesus did not set apart special times for prayer. He lived in the constant presence of God the Father. He continued to refer to his Father in a very intimate way using a very homely word for God. He taught his disciples to share in this intimate and unique relationship. He taught them to pray by his life, he taught them of life in parables.

5. The Parables

How do we interpret the parables? Much has been written and many attempts have been made to find a pattern that would allow us to understand them fully. They have always been recognized as central to the teaching of Jesus and though they have been reshaped in transmission we often feel we are close to the mind of Jesus as we ponder their meaning.

The traditional interpretation of the parables was that they were addressed to the whole Church throughout the ages. Often treated as allegories, they were used to illustrate some current situation. They were seen as a type of prophecy by Jesus of things to come. This approach seems to have been adopted early in the life of the Church. Those who wrote the gospels made some of the parables apply to their own day. The interpretation of the parable of the Sower may have been added by the evangelists to make the parable refer to those who had fallen away from the Christian faith even at that early date.

In the post-New Testament period the allegorical interpretation of the parables became increasingly popular. For Tertullian, the Prodigal Son is the Christian, the elder son the Jew. The share of property claimed is the knowledge of God. The far country is the land of the devil. The feast on the return of the prodigal is the eucharist. The fatted calf the Saviour.[112]

The ingenuity of some of these interpretations is truly astounding and the allegorical method remained the standard way of explaining the parables until relatively recent times, despite the protests of the reformers. Archbishop Trench, in his famous book *Notes on the Parables,* first printed in 1841, follows the reformers teaching when expounding the parable of the Good Samaritan.[113] He gives the plain meaning of the text. Then he says "Beautiful as is this parable when thus taken simply in the letter, inviting us to 'put on bowels of mercies,' to shrink from no offices of love, even though they should be painful and perilous; yet how much fairer still, how much more mightily provoking to love and good works, when, with most of the Fathers, and with many of the Reformers, we trace in it a deeper meaning still, and see the work of Christ, the merciful Son of Man Himself, portrayed to us here." The interpretation he then develops can be traced back, through the Reformation, through the Middle Ages, to Augustine and then on to Origen.

The book that changed the interpretation of the parables was published in Germany almost fifty years after the publication of Trench's book. Adolph Jülicher in his work *Die Gleichnisreden Jesu'* (Vol. 1, 1888, Vol. 2, 1899)[114] showed that parables in general do not admit of an allegorical interpretation and that the interpretations added by the evangelists rest on a misunderstanding. He taught that the parables make one central point and that Jesus used them to make his message plain. The suggestion that Jesus used parables so that people would not understand (Mk. 4.11, par.) was seen by Jülicher as a teaching of the early Church.

Although Jülicher cleared away misconceptions of the past, he considered the parables to be little more than the expression of simple moral truths. It is difficult to believe that Jesus would have been brought to crucifixion if he was only a pietistic preacher. Our present understanding of the parables has been formed by two books, C.H. Dodd's *Parables of the Kingdom* (1935)[115] and Joachim Jeremias' *Parables of Jesus* (1947).[116] In these books the parables are seen, with the miracles, as part of Jesus' great proclamation that the kingdom of God was breaking into history. This modern scholarship has sought to place the parables in the same context as that in which they were delivered by Jesus. The second section of Jeremias' book, entitled "The Return to Jesus from the Primitive Church" shows how the parables have been changed by their translation into Greek, by embellishment, by the change of audience, by the delay of the parousia and by other factors. Summing up this section of the book, Jeremias says: "The parables have a twofold historical setting. First, the original historical setting, not only of the parables, but of all the sayings of Jesus, in their individual concrete situation in the activity of Jesus. Then there is a second historical setting, which is the situation of the primitive Church. We only know the parables in the form in which they were received from the primitive Church; hence we are faced with the task of recovering their original form in so far as that is possible for us."[117]

The parables are then to be seen as independent units set in a framework supplied by the gospel writers. Sometimes the setting supplied by the evangelist will be useful in understanding the parable, sometimes, when different settings are supplied for the same parable, a judgement is needed as to which of the settings supplied best fits the life and teaching of Jesus. Sometimes a parable will need to be considered apart from the supplied setting. The picture that is often sketched is of Jesus as a preacher using the parables to illustrate a point that he is making to "the crowds that followed."

Jeremias does not go beyond attempting to discover the "original form" of the parables to consider what would have been their original setting. In the third section of his book he divides the parables by looking at their message.[118] He gives a clear setting to one group of parables in the section of his book entitled "Realized Discipleship." Here he shows how Jesus trained the disciples by parables.

First, Jesus taught the disciples that "the measure of mercy is in force at the Last Judgement."[119] According to Jeremias this is the point of the Good Samaritan (Lk. 10.25–37), the description of the sentence pronounced at the Last Judgement, (Matt. 25.31–46) and the parable of the Unmerciful Servant.

The second characteristic of what Jeremias calls "the little flock," most strongly emphasized in Jesus' metaphors, is the absolute security that the disciples have as God's chosen. They have "a Father who cares for them and, moreover, they have a Master who calls them by name as a shepherd does his sheep" (Jn. 10.3).[120]

The third characteristic of the discipleship, which Jesus taught by parables and similes was a call to action. Jesus calls the disciples to be fishers of men (Mk. 1.17), to be laborers of the harvest (Matt. 9.37), to be shepherds of the flock (Matt. 10.6). As his messengers they have judicial authority (Matt. 16.19, 18.18).

Our suggestion is that all the parables must be seen as having been directed originally at the disciples. They are neither revelations of things to come for Christians down the ages, nor are they to be used, as they have been used by the evangelists, to deal with problems faced in their own day and in their own Church tradition, nor are they illustrations from sermons preached by Jesus to "the crowds." The parables are what has survived of the teaching method used by Jesus with his disciples. This would explain why so many of the parables have survived as independent units. It wasn't that the disciples remembered the teaching of Jesus addressed to the crowds. The disciples remembered the teaching that was directed at them.

In Mark 4.10–12, Jesus is with his small group of followers. They ask him about his method of teaching. He replies, "To you has been given the secret of the kingdom of God, but to those outside everything is in parables." We cannot believe that Jesus did not desire to be understood by the people and therefore taught in puzzling riddles. If we accept the saying without the allegorical interpretation added by the evangelists to explain why the Jewish people rejected Jesus, we are left with a statement of fact. Only the inner circle, only the small group was able to understand the parabolic teaching of Jesus. The same point is made by Jesus in Luke 12.41f. Peter asks, "Lord are you telling this parable for us or for all?" Jesus replies with the parable of the Faithful Steward. Luke then has the passage "I came to cast fire upon the earth; and would that it were already kindled." Jesus then goes on to speak about divisions among families. Rather different versions of this saying occur in Mark 13.12 and Matthew 10.34. All three evangelists see this passage as a prediction by Jesus of dire things to come, as a prediction of his death, of the persecution of the disciples, of the Roman war. Mark uses it as a forecast of the division among families at a time of persecution. If we accept that the passage was addressed to the twelve, we can see that Luke is correct in seeing it as the answer to Peter's question. Jesus saw his ministry as moving to a crisis but the division among families had already taken place. It had happened with his own friends, they had thought him mad (Mk. 3.21). It must have also happened within the families of many of the members of the small group about Jesus. Their decision to follow Jesus must have led to dissension and division. Understood in this way the passage may be seen to refer directly to the situation faced by Jesus and his close disciples.

Many of the difficulties in the interpretation of the parables disappear if they are understood in this way. For instance, the parable of the Wicked Husbandmen (Mk. 12.1–12, par.) has, since the time of Jülicher,[121] been understood by many scholars as an allegorical construction of the early Church. They suggest that we see the owner to be God, the vineyard Israel, the husbandmen the Jewish leaders, the servants the Old Testament prophets. Thus the son of the owner is Jesus and the destruction at the end a reference to the end of the Jewish state. The reason this interpretation of the parable is so attractive is that it is hard to imagine why else Jesus would tell this detailed and rather improbable story in which he claims to be the son of God and attributes his own death to "the chief priests and the scribes and the elders" (Mk. 11.27). John Drury in his recent book *The Parables in the Gospels* agrees with this explanation and tells us that this allegory "is the whole of the history which concerned Mark as the origin and authentification of his religion. It extends from the beginnings of Israel to the fall of Jerusalem in AD 70 and the rise of gentile Christianity."[122]

C.H. Dodd rejects the suggestion that the parable is an allegory. He finds that this "most difficult of parables" reflects the situation in the countryside at the time of Jesus. He calls the parable "natural and realistic in every way."[123] He tells us that the natural ending of the parable is the question "what will the owner of the vineyard do?" (Mk. 12.9). The progressive elaboration that we see applied to the parable, especially in Matthew and Luke, only shows that the early Church held this parable to be of peculiar importance. The number of "servants" may have been increased to suggest the long role of prophets. With these changes he believes that the parable "stands on its own feet as a dramatic story" and may, in this more simple form, have challenged the public of Jerusalem "to recognize the more than prophetic character of His mission."[124]

The difficulty with this suggestion is that such a parable, addressed to the public, would be seen by the authorities in Jerusalem as a challenge by Jesus to kill him as they had killed prophets before him. If, on the other hand, the parable was first heard by Jesus' close disciples, it becomes much more acceptable as it stands. A shorter version of the parable was probably told to the disciples as the events that led up to the crucifixion began to come together. Jesus used the model of the violent fate of the prophets to explain to his close disciples their involvement in the final crisis of God's dealing with his people Israel. This parable, like the "Q" passages that speak of Jerusalem as the place that slew the prophets (Matt. 23.27–39, par.) was part of the preparation of the disciples for death and martyrdom.

We do not intend to make a complete study of the parables, but only to demonstrate that they are best understood as being directed originally to the small group about Jesus. Understood in this way the parables fall into three groups. Many were originally told to encourage the twelve. They were parables explaining to the disciples their situation and warning them of the difficulties they would face in the days to come. Then there were parables that must be seen as reflecting some comment originally made by Jesus to the disciples on the state of Judaism. Jesus also used parables to explain God's plan for their world. All the parables of Jesus can be placed in one of these three categories.

First, let us consider those parables that were originally used by Jesus to encourage, to warn and support the small group about him. The twelve faced doubts and disappointments in their decision to follow Jesus. Many of the parables were told so that the disciples could better understand their role. The little parable of the Leaven (Matt. 13.33, Lk. 13.20, 21) is an apt illustration of the ministry of Jesus and the disciples. They were the leaven in the lump of Israel. Perhaps when the parable was told there was little happening. Yet soon the swelling and the bubbling would begin. In the twin parables of the Treasure and the Pearl, a peasant stumbles upon a treasure hidden in a field and a merchant comes upon a priceless pearl. Both act quickly if dishonestly. They gain the prize. Many would have thought the disciples rash when they followed Jesus but they too had seized the opportunity to gain the prize.

The parable of the laborers in the Vineyard (Matt. 20.1–16) has had many interpretations down the ages. Dodd tells us that the "setting in life" of this parable is a retort of Jesus to "the complaints of the legally minded who cavilled at him as a friend of publicans and sinners."[125] Those hired in the last hour then, are they of no value to God. The story tells of a generous employer who treats those who worked a short time as those who had worked the long day. Our suggestion is that this parable told the disciples something of divine generosity. They must have wondered how they could have been so privileged as to be laborers in God's vineyard in such a late hour. Jesus saw his ministry as the culmination of all that had gone before, as the fulfillment of the Law and the Prophets. This ministry would last but a short time, yet they would be treated as equals of Moses and Elijah.

There are other parables of the countryside that were told to encourage the disciples. The parable of the Seed Growing Secretly (Mk. 4.26–29), like the parable of the Leaven told of a natural process. It was a way of explaining what was taking place to the disciples. They were among the few who would labor in the harvest, when the crop was ripe. We have the same message in a saying of Jesus, "The harvest is plentiful but the laborers few" (Matt. 9.37, Lk. 10.2). The parable of the Sower (Mk. 4.3f), culled of its interpretation, tells us of a farmer who in spite of bare patches has a great harvest. Again the disciples are being told that in spite of the mixture of failure and success in Galilee, they will come to see the "restoration of all things" (Mk. 9.12). We have two variant traditions of the parable of the Great Feast (Matt. 22.1–13, Lk. 14.16–24). The disciples would have recognized the symbol of the heavenly banquet. They had been promised that "many will come from east and west and sit at table with Abraham, Isaac and Jacob in the kingdom of heaven" (Matt. 8.11). They were to help carry the invitation abroad, and would find that many of the invited would reject the invitation. Their task was to "take heed, watch," like the servants in the parable of the Waiting Servants (Mk. 13.33–37, Lk. 12.35–40) or the Ten Virgins in Matthew's parable (Matt. 25.1–12). These parables have been greatly elaborated yet their message is simple. They were told to encourage the disciples, as Jesus encouraged Peter at Gethsemane to "Watch and pray, that you might not enter into temptation" (Mk. 14.38).

In another group of parables, Jesus taught the disciples to understand the religious affairs of their time. The little parable of the Children in the Marketplace (Matt. 11.16–19, Lk. 7.31–35) is followed by a passage that comments on the frivolous attitude of the majority of people to the words of John and Jesus. There is a similar parabolic saying in Mark 2.18, 19. The disciples are attacked because they do not fast. Jesus replies, "Can the wedding guests fast while the bridegroom is with them?" Wedding attendants were released from some religious obligations so that they could rejoice. Jesus suggests to his disciples that they are likewise released from religious obligation. Mark added a pair of parables to this discussion. Both the parable of the Patched Garment and the parable of the Old Wineskins (Mk. 2.21, 22) suggest that it is a mistake to try repairing something that is worn out. The old and the new are incompatible. Jesus was not calling for the reform of Israel, it was past reform. The twelve were to be part of a new age. In this new age they were, like the wedding guests, free to share in a time of feasting and celebration.

The little parable of the Salt is found in the synoptics (Mk. 9.50, Matt. 5.13, Lk. 14.34, 35). The setting and the application are different in all three gospels. It seems that the early Church remembered the parable but did not remember how the parable was originally applied. If we take the parable as it stands we have a comment on something that was once valuable that has now lost its value. Jesus saw the Judaism of his time in just this way. Thus we have his comment to the disciples on the religious authorities. Matthew perhaps understood this because when he came to write he changed the application of the parable from the negative to the positive, from Judaism to the disciples. He has Jesus tell the disciples "You are the salt of the earth." If Judaism is the decayed salt, Matthew saw that the salt that will purify and preserve Israel was the sacrifice of the twelve. In the parable of the Lamp, we again have a different application in each of the synoptics (Mk. 4.21, Matt. 5.15, Lk. 8.16). If we take this parable as it stands, we have a comment by Jesus to the disciples on the religious leaders of Judaism. They had hidden the light of God. Their interest was in saving God's light for themselves. The task of the disciples was to show that light to all the world. The parable of the Strong Man (Mk. 3.27, Matt. 12.24–29, Lk. 11.21, 22) is set by all three writers in passages that deal with exorcism. In both Luke and Matthew the meaning is made clear by the saying "But if it is by the finger of God (the Spirit of God in Matthew) that I cast out demons, then the kingdom of God has come upon you" (Lk. 11.20). The power of Jesus and his disciples over demons is a sign that the end-time is upon them. This parable tells the disciples that their task is to bind the strong man, Satan. The parable of the Wicked Husbandmen (Mk. 12.1–12, Matt. 21.33–46, Lk. 20.9–19) tells of a landlord's difficulties with his tenants. The disciples, knowing Isaiah's Song of the Beloved (Isa. 5.1, 2) would have understood this parable as an attack on the rulers of the nation. The parable has been expanded because of its openness to allegorical interpretation, the servants become the prophets, the "beloved son" becomes Jesus. In the simple, original form the parable must be seen as a comment on leaders of Judaism.

Another parable that lent itself to an allegorical interpretation is the parable of the Talents (Matt. 25.14-30, Lk. 19.12-27). The evangelists see this parable as an exhortation to Christians to be diligent in their religious life while they await the second advent. If we remember that the basic story is of a man giving money in trust for other to invest and then after a time calling them to account for their investments, we can see that the cautious investor is the target of the story. What he has will be taken from him. Again, we have a comment by Jesus to the disciples on the over-cautious leaders of Judaism who would keep the knowledge of God to themselves and not "risk their capital."

Our third group of parables are those that were used by Jesus to teach the disciples about God, about his kingdom and the new age to come. The parable of the Tares (Matt. 13.24–30) is used by Matthew to suggest that, although there may be good and bad members of the Church, nothing should be done to excommunicate them until God judges them at the final judgement. If we refer the parable to the time of Jesus and the disciples, we can see that Jesus must have used the parable to explain to the disciples God's action in bringing the kingdom. The kingdom of God would not be delayed because there were still evil people. Just as a farmer does not delay his harvest because of a few weeds, so God will not delay the coming of the kingdom because there are still sinners in Israel. Another parable found in Matthew (Matt. 13.47, 48) is the parable of the Dragnet. As it stands in the gospel it is a parable that tells of the day of judgement. If we see it as told to the disciples it becomes a reminder that as fishers of men they must gather in every type of person.

Luke has a group of three parables in a setting that has Jesus and his group dining with many "publicans and sinners." These are the parables of the Lost Sheep (Lk. 15.3–7), the Lost Coin (Lk. 15.8–10) and the Prodigal Son (Lk. 15.11–14). The parable of the Lost Sheep appears in Matthew (Matt. 18.12–14) in another setting with a different "moral." Luke uses these parables to show the concern of Jesus for those outside the religious community. The stories of the Lost Sheep and the Lost Coin show the concern a person can have for what others would ignore. We can see this in these three parables. In them Jesus told the disciples that God was just like these searchers. He cared for the lost. The Prodigal Son, in a different way, has the same message. The delight of the father over the return of the son he had lost may have upset his older brother, but was this not exactly what was happening in Israel?

A parable that appears in Matthew (Matt. 24.45–51) and with little variation in Luke (Lk. 12.39–46) brings our short survey of the parables to a close. It could be called the parable of the Faithful and the Unfaithful Servants. The evangelists see this story as a parable of the second advent. This could not have been the theme when it was told by Jesus. Those who heard him knew nothing about a second advent. They did know that Israel was often thought of as the servant of God. Isaiah and some of the Psalms had used the image. The disciples would have known who Jesus was calling the unfaithful servants. They were the religious leaders of the time. They also knew that Jesus was calling them to be the faithful servants who would be set to judge the twelve tribes of Israel.

In a sense we have been stating the obvious. All would agree that the parables were first told in the presence of the twelve. Yet, more than that, they must be understood as being directed completely at the encouragement and enlightenment of the twelve. When those outside the group could not understand the parables they protested, hence the saying: "To you has been given the secret of the kingdom of God, but for those outside everything is in parables" (Mk. 4.11). Only the small group could understand the teaching. There were other teachings of Jesus that have come down to us as "sayings." We turn to study these "sayings" in our next chapter.

6. A Rule of Life

There is nothing in the gospels like a rule of life. The nearest we approach such an ethical system is the gathering together by Matthew and Luke of the "sayings" of Jesus in what have come to be known as "the Sermon on the Mount" (Matt. 5.3–7.28) and "the Sermon on the Plain" (Lk. 6.17–49).

These sayings have been used by many to confirm their own point of view. Karl Bornhäuser, in his book *Die Bergpredigt*,[126] argues that the Sermon on the Mount must be understood as it would have been understood by a Jewish contemporary of Jesus. If we did this we would no

longer call it a "sermon." We would call it "the Teaching on the
Mount" for it does not contain gospel preaching but disciple teaching.
In the haggadic tradition Jesus gives his disciples "Halachot," a guide
for living, telling them what is to be done, how they are to live. What he
gives them is not something for future contemplation, it is to be enacted
immediately. Bornhäuser tells us that "These words are taught in order
that they may be obeyed, and immediately at that, under the prevailing
circumstances of the time. The fulfillment of this demand is expected
only from Jesus' disciples."[127] All through these passages it is the disciples who are contrasted with the Pharisaic scribes, not the masses. It is
from the twelve disciples that Jesus demands a higher righteousness.[128] In
this Jesus follows the normal rabbinic attitude that says that thought and
deed are inseparable.

Both at the beginning and at the end of the Sermon on the Mount
"crowds" are mentioned. It is implied that the sermon was addressed to
them. If we look more closely at the opening verse we see that the
sermon is addressed to the disciples. "Seeing the crowds, he went up on
the mountain, and when he sat down his disciples came to him and he
opened his mouth and taught them" (Matt. 5.1). We usually read this
verse to mean that the crowds followed Jesus up the mountain. It could
mean that he went to the mountain to avoid the crowds. The verse does
make clear that the sermon was addressed to the disciples alone. "He
opened his mouth and taught them." Jesus is seated with the disciples
about him in the traditional setting for a teacher giving a lesson. We
have a similar setting in Luke. After the appointment of the twelve (Lk.
6.12–16), Jesus and his small group of disciples come down to a level
place. Great crowds are attracted from a wide area to hear Jesus preach
and to watch him heal the sick. Then "he lifted up his eyes on his disciples and said... " (Lk. 6.20). The Sermon on the Plain was directed at
"the disciples."

Both Matthew and Luke attempt to give their "sermons" a universal
application. Matthew ends his sermon with the words "the crowds were
astonished at his teaching" (Matt. 7.28). Yet both evangelists make it
clear that the teaching in the "sermons" was originally directed at the
twelve.[129]

Many of the difficulties that commentators have had with these passages have been caused by the failure to understand that the teachings
were originally an important part of the training of the twelve. Here we
have an ethic that tore a person loose from family friends and all of society; an ethic that expected heroic sacrifice; an ethic that was centered

only on the individual and the individual's preparation for the coming kingdom. Here was an ethic that ruled out the consideration of other values, other interests, other people. How can it be that the meek "shall inherit the earth" (Matt. 5.5)? Can it be wrong to swear an oath (Matt. 5.33–37)? Can it be wrong to resist evil (Matt. 5.38–42)? How can Jesus demand that all society "be perfect, as your heavenly Father is perfect" (Matt. 5.48). Most people find the passage about possessions difficult to accept (Matt. 6.19–21). But Jesus makes this choice absolute, "You cannot serve God and mammon" (Matt. 6.24). The passage about the "narrow gate" suggests that very few will find "life" (Matt. 7.13, 14). Literally interpreted and applied to all, this rule seems absurd, impossible, extravagant.

Matthew's version begins with a series of beatitudes. They describe the blessedness of the disciples who have come under the Father's rule as made manifest by Jesus. This preface tells us that the ideal disciple is poor, meek and lowly in heart. They are people who mourn for God's people, mourn for the evil of the world, who hunger for righteousness and are prepared to suffer for its triumph. They are merciful and pure of heart. They are peacemakers, those who reconcile others and develop harmony. All these words recall words of messianic promise. The disciples, by God's gracious goodness, have been called to share in the fulfillment of these promises. They are like salt, that tiny grain that makes such a difference. They are the opposite of the religious leaders of Judaism who have become like savorless salt. They are like a light set out on a stand, "a light to the nations that my salvation may reach the ends of the earth" (Isa. 49.6). Like a city on a hill they will not remain obscure. One result is that they will be reviled and persecuted. They will suffer like the prophets of old and like those prophets people will come to see the good that they do and they will give glory to their Father in heaven. Jesus also insists that they fulfill the letter of the law, that they go beyond the Pharisees to meet its requirements (Matt. 5.18–20).

Bornhäuser makes the point that the beatitudes are not to be spiritualized. They apply to a special historical situation. He suggests that in blessing the poor, Jesus is addressing the economic problems of the times. His first beatitude, like his temple cleansing, attacks the sanction that had been put on the exploitation of the poor by the religious leaders of the day.[130]

In the next section (Matt. 5.21–26), Jesus warns the disciples about violent argument. "Everyone who is angry with his brother shall be liable to judgement; whoever insults his brother shall be liable to the council, and whoever says, 'You fool' shall be liable to the hell of fire." If a dispute arose among them they must settle that dispute immediately. They must not become involved in the Jewish justice system. In taking this attitude Jesus was endorsing the mild attitude of Hillel over the haughty attitude of Shammai. Where some of the disciples of the Pharisees took great delight in personal disputes, Jesus tells his disciples, the teachers of his new community, that they must live in harmony, forbearing one another.

Jesus also tells his disciples that they must control their sexual desires (Matt. 5.27–32). They must not let one part of their body rule their life. The passage that speaks of looking on a women lustfully as adultery goes on to say, "If your right eye causes you to sin, pluck it out and throw it away; it is better that you lose one of your members than that your whole body is thrown into hell" (Matt. 5.29). There is a similar passage in Matthew 19.12 where Jesus speaks of those who have been eunuchs from birth or by human hand and those who have become eunuchs for the sake of the kingdom of heaven. In this passage Jesus tells the disciples "he who is able to receive this, let him receive it." We can assume that many of the disciples were married. At that time most people married at an early age. Paul claims the right to be accompanied by a wife "as the other apostles and the brothers of the Lord and Cephas" (1 Cor. 9.5). Some of the disciples may have wished to divorce their wives so that they would be free to be with Jesus. They may have thought it the right thing to do, but Jesus forbids divorce. He tells the disciples that a divorce would make the woman an adulteress. The passage about divorce had immediate application. In this passage then, Jesus counsels his disciples about their relationship to their wives and to other women. Bornhäuser makes the point that the rabbis taught their disciples to avoid speaking to women and to try not to look at them. The faithful were to shut their eyes on meeting a woman in public and in this way they would be able to retain their pure intentions and continue to meditate on the law.[131] Jesus rejects this attitude. He did not presume that a woman was an evil object.

The injunction "Do not swear at all" (Matt. 5.34) also had an immediate application. All the oaths mentioned were used by the religious people of the time. Oriental hyperbole often led to exaggeration. Like the Essenes, Jesus rejected the practice. His disciples must speak plainly one to another.

The section on retaliation (Matt. 5.38–42) is easier to understand if it was directed solely to the disciples. It is hard to believe that Jesus required that all who accept him should not resist "one who is evil." In the time of Jesus the formula "an eye for an eye" had been codified in a civil formula of indemnification. All the situations mentioned would result in a disciple becoming involved in legal proceedings. Far better to give way, there were more important things at hand. Jesus is telling them to forego their legal claims to justice while they are his disciples.

Bornhäuser points out that this text "Resist not evil" allowed Tolstoy to go to battle against war in the name of Jesus. This was only possible because Tolstoy failed completely to understand the specific civil-juridical context of the passage.[132] We can only understand this text when we realize that the established civil practice of indemnification for personal injury, as later codified in the Mishnah, which applied to the scribes, was not allowed by Jesus for his disciples. The proper way to translate that passage therefore would be to paraphrase it as "You, (my disciple) shall not go to court with the evil one."

Bornhäuser goes on to say that it is unjust to think the Pharisees taught "resist, go to court, retaliate." All that Jesus said had been said by Pharisaic scribes. The difference is in how these demands apply.[133] The Pharisees counselled restraint in pursuing one's rights, especially if injured or insulted by a colleague. This magnanimity in foregoing one's rightful claim to justice, contemplated under some circumstances by the scribes, was required by Jesus from his disciples even when faced by an "evildoer."[134]

The next section (Matt. 5.43–48) must be seen in its contemporary context. In Israel, for generations, religious teachers had looked down on those who were outside the law or ignorant of its precepts. Jesus calls for a complete reversal of this attitude. God treats everyone equally. So must the disciples of Jesus. One of the attractions of living apart in a religious group is the appeal of perfection. Jesus tells the twelve that "You therefore, must be perfect, as your heavenly Father is perfect, you must love and respect all peoples."

Our study of the devotional life of Jesus and his disciples has shown how Jesus rejected the set forms of spiritual exercise, almsgivings, prayer and fasting, which were the outward marks of most religious groups. His teaching on the devotional life is connected with the next section of this rule of life (Matt. 6.1–34). Jesus warns the disciples about the dangers of money and possessions. The disciples must not teach for profit as some religious teachers of the time, nor must they work at their trades. They are to trust God for their needs. Like the birds and the lilies they are not to face the anxiety of providing for their own needs. Poverty is not a fate but a calling. They were to live totally dependent on those who would furnish God's provisions.

The problem caused when religious teachers become involved in a trade and in gathering possessions was much debated in the Judaism of this time. Jesus was not the first to declare, "You received without pay, give without pay" (Matt. 10.8). Rabbis were also forbidden by the *Torah* to profit from their teaching. Yet it seems there were scribes who would "devour widows' houses" (Mk. 12.40, Lk. 20.47). Jesus will not have them as an example for his disciples; they are not to do as the scribes do, for the scribes "preach but do not practice" (Matt. 23.16, 17). Jesus declares that his disciples are released from the responsibility of possessions and the duty of earning a living. They are to sell what they have and give the proceeds to the poor (Lk. 12.33). The Rich Young Man could not be his disciple because he had great possessions and he could not bring himself to part with them (Mk. 10.17–31, par.).

Bornhäuser suggests that the word we usually translate "to be anxious" in this section of the "sermon" should really be translated "to labor" and that it is therefore a synonym for "to toil" in Matthew 6.28.[135] The word is used in this way in the Septuagint to refer to the labor required of the Israelites by Pharaoh (Ex. 5.9). In Luke 10.41, Martha is reprimanded by Jesus not for being "anxious" but for "working." It follows that the passage that we usually translate "and why are you anxious about clothing?" (Matt. 6.28), is not about the possession of clothing or even their style or fashion, the question is "Why are you toiling for clothing?" The passage goes on "Consider the lilies of the field, how they grow, they neither toil or spin... But if God so clothes the grass of the field... will he not much more clothe you?" (Matt. 6.28–30). The point of Matthew 6.25–34 is not that all Christians should stop being anxious and being worried, but that the disciples free themselves from all that is entailed in following a trade and owning material possessions. As Paul put it, "the Lord commanded that those who proclaim the gospel should get their living by the gospel" (1 Cor. 9.14).

The final section, Chapter 7, is in the form of an exhortation. The disciples must be true to their calling. They must not judge each other, nor waste their time with the worthless, those who would be called dogs or pigs. They are to trust their heavenly Father who gives good gifts to his children. They will find that they only have to ask and they will receive, to knock at a door and it will be opened. They are the few who have entered the narrow gate and begun to walk the hard path but they have chosen the way of life (Jer. 21.8).

Jesus warns his disciples to beware of false prophets. They are like bad trees that bear bad fruit. There are other teachers who claim to be disciples of Jesus. They prophesy in his name, they cast out demons, they do "mighty works." We find similar references to these others who would claim to be disciples of Jesus in a parallel passage in Luke 6.46 and in Luke 13.25–27 and Matthew 25.41–46. Jesus rejects them as his disciples. The small group that Jesus has chosen to be "with him" are not to be confused with others who would claim the privileges that they have been given. Jesus tells them that it is their task to do the will of his heavenly Father (Matt. 7.21).

Both versions of the sermon end with the parable of the house built on the sand and the house built on the rock. The promise given the group by Jesus is that they will be built on the rock as the wise man builds his house.

The Sermon on the Mount is a summary of the teaching that Jesus gave the group that he had formed to share in his ministry. This teaching was given at a time of intense religious ferment. Every reference becomes clear if we see this teaching as the instruction given to the disciples. It was their training for ministry, it was to be their rule of life. When the evangelists came to write they tried to make this teaching apply to the whole Church, yet its original purpose shines through. The teaching often becomes impossible when generalized and applied to situations outside its original setting. The friendship that Jesus showed to "sinners" also becomes understandable when we see that friendship in its original setting.

7. Forgiveness

"Beginning with Moses and all the prophets he interpreted to them in all the scriptures the things concerning himself" (Lk. 24.27). For those two disciples on that walk to Emmaus and for those early Christians who read St. Luke, the central aspect of this new understanding of scripture as taught by Jesus was the forgiveness of sins.

Sin came from breaking the law of God. Such an action often brought suffering (Jn. 9.2) as punishment. Every person owed full obedience to God and every failure to achieve such obedience to the Law puts that person at risk. The sacrificial cult of Israel was developed over the centuries to allow these debts to be paid, these separations from the law of God to be ended, these sins to be forgiven.[136] Any study of the Old Testament sacrificial system has to be complex and difficult because of the many revisions of ancient traditions. The object of some sacrifices was to end the division between God and man, to bring them into fellowship or communion. In such a sacrifice the animal was at times shared, partly eaten by the worshipper, partly burnt at the altar and thereby given to God. These can be called freewill offerings, thank-offerings, votive offerings (Lev. 22.18f).[137] The great prophets protested that none of these rituals alone, without the right intention, were to any purpose. The sacrificial system was not magic. To obtain fellowship with God, to give him gifts, to receive forgiveness, one must share in the system truly and honestly from the heart (Amos 4.4, 5, 5.21–24, Isa. 1.10–15, Jer. 7.21–26).

In the days before the exile, while Israel prospered, the system was respected and revered. With the exile and the troubled times that followed, the efficacy of the whole system was at times called into question. The Prophets had taught that only a people pure and loyal to God could offer true sacrifice. Because people despaired of ever meeting the requirements for true sacrifice and so obtain forgiveness, the annual ceremony known as the Day of Atonement grew in importance (Lev. 16).[138] By the time of Jesus, the Temple sacrifice called "sin" or "trespass" or "guilt offering," ritual cleansing and works of supererogation such as almsgiving were common practice for the religious minded. Yet Israel suffered, controlled by a foreign power, ruled by gentiles or those who made themselves to be gentiles, the quislings of Jewish society.

Into this situation came "a man sent from God, whose name was John" (Jn. 1.6). Mark tells us that "John the Baptizer appeared in the wilderness preaching a baptism of repentance for the forgiveness of sins" (Mk. 1.4). A passage in Luke tells us that he called on those who came out to him to change their ways, to share their goods with the poor, to extort no more and not to be violent. He told soldiers to be content with their wages (Lk. 3.13, 14). A "Q" passage tells us that he called on people to "bear fruit that befits repentance" (Matt. 3.8, Lk. 3.8). Passages in Mark and Matthew tell us that people were baptized "confessing their sins" (Mk. 1.5, Matt. 3.6). This picture of John that we have from the gospels is confirmed by Josephus.[139] He explains that baptism served to purify the body of a person whose soul had first been purified by righteousness. He does not mention John's eschatological preaching, that as "Q" puts it "now the axe is laid to the root of the tree" (Matt. 3.10, Lk. 3.9) but this may have been because he did not wish to mention messianism in his writings.[140] In his teaching John emphasized that people should repent and then the end would come. He followed the prophets who taught that if in Israel, "the wicked forsook his way and the unrighteousness man his thoughts... soon my salvation would come and my deliverance be revealed" (Isa. 55.7–56.1).

It is much more difficult to discern the teaching of Jesus on repentance. His teaching also had a background in the Old Testament, in prophets who emphasized the action of God. In Jeremiah we are told: "Behold I will bring to it health and healing, and I will heal them and reveal to them the abundance of prosperity and security. I will restore the fortunes of Judah and the fortunes of Israel, and rebuild them as they were at first. I will cleanse them from all the guilt of their sin against me, and I will forgive all the guilt of their sin and rebellion against me" (Jer. 33.6–8). So in the book of Ezekiel, the people who should be the shepherds of the people are condemned, they have been feeding themselves rather than feeding the sheep. Therefore God promises that he will come himself: "I will save my flock, they shall no longer be a prey; and I will judge between sheep and sheep. And I will set up over them one shepherd, my servant David, and he shall feed them and be their shepherd. And I, the Lord, will be their God, and my servant David shall be Prince among them" (Ezek. 34.22–24). Instead of John's promise that if people would repent the end would come, Jesus seems to have promised that the end would come, and indeed was at hand. Then would come judgement and repentance. "As for you, my flock, thus says the Lord God; Behold, I judge between sheep and sheep, rams and he-goats" (Ezek. 34.17). Just as, "all the tribes of Israel came to David at Hebron and said, Behold, we are your bone and flesh. In times past, when Saul was king over us, it was you that led out and brought in Israel; and the Lord said to you, You shall be shepherd of my people of Israel, and you shall be prince over Israel" (2 Sam. 5.1-3). So now, Jesus, "Son of David" led out and brought Israel and appointed those who would help him shepherd and judge Israel.

Jesus associated his ministry with that of John the Baptist, indeed John's gospel tells us that he drew his first disciples from the ranks of the Baptist's followers (Jn. 1.35–40). Yet all the gospels affirm that the ministry of Jesus was very different from that of the Baptist. John was a fasting (Mk. 2.18f) ascetic (Mk. 1.6, par.) who called people to the desert to separate the wheat from the chaff (Matt. 3.12, Lk. 3.17). Jesus was known as a winebibber and glutton (Matt. 11.19, par.) who associated with "sinners and tax collectors" (Mk. 2.16, par.).

E.P. Sanders in his book *Jesus and Judaism* suggests that the greatest difference between the Baptist's teaching and Jesus' teaching is that "there is not a single solid piece of information about Jesus that indicates that he was . . . one who called for general repentance in view of the coming kingdom."[141] Sanders sees the statement in Mark 1.15f and par. as much more the teaching of the early Church about Jesus than a summary of the actual teaching of Jesus. He points out that there are only a few passages that link repentance to the coming of the kingdom. Two of these passages are from "Q," (Matt. 11.21–24, Lk. 10.13–15, Matt. 12.38–42, Lk. 11.29–32) and one passage is from Luke (3.1–5). They tell of repentant gentiles while the people of Israel remain unrepentant. Sanders claims that this is again the work of the early Church. Aside from passages and sayings that seem to be editorial (Mk. 6.12, Lk. 5.32, par., Matt. 4.17, par.) there seems to be very little that can be attributed to Jesus about repentance. In spite of Luke's conclusion, the parable about the lost sheep is about God's action, not about repentance (Lk. 15.3–10).

Jesus did not call for a general repentance because the kingdom was at hand. He announced (Lk. 7.47–49) individual forgiveness to some (Matt. 9.2–6, par.), he called on people to forgive one another (Matt. 18.21f, par.). Blasphemy against the Holy Spirit would not be forgiven (Matt. 12.31f, par.). The small group of disciples was taught to pray for forgiveness (Matt. 6.12, 14, par.). Jesus prays for the forgiveness of his executioners (Lk. 23.34). He told parables about repentance and forgiveness (Lk. 15.3–10, 15.11–32, 18.9–14) All this was part of the coming of the rule of God, the coming of the kingdom.

According to Matthew 26.28, at the last supper that Jesus had with his small group of disciples, he taught them "this is the blood of the covenant which is poured out for many for the forgiveness of sins." The phrase "for the forgiveness of sins" is probably not authentic. It does not appear in the parallels nor in 1 Cor. 11.23–25. Yet Matthew may well have understood what happened at that last meal when he added that passage. Jesus told the disciples "I will not drink again of the fruit of the vine until that day when I drink it new with you in my Father's kingdom" (Matt. 26.29, par.). Jesus looked to God to bring the end, to bring judgement, repentance and forgiveness, when, as the Psalm of Solomon puts it, the Davidic King shall "not suffer unrighteousness to lodge any more in their midst" (Ps. of Sol. 17.20). On that day, with his small group, Jesus looked to cleanse, purify, judge, heal and forgive.

In Matthew 19.28, Jesus promises Peter and the disciples "Truly, I say to you, in the new world, when the Son of Man shall sit on his glorious throne, you who have followed me will also sit on twelve thrones, judging the twelve tribes of Israel." In Luke 22.30, the promise is that "you may eat and drink at my table in my kingdom, and sit on thrones judging the twelve tribes of Israel." There is good reason to believe that the promise that the disciples would sit in judgement is authentic. The promise of an event that the early Church thought was yet to take place (Rev. 21.12f), the promise of an event that would "enthrone" the disciple who had betrayed Jesus would be a very strange invention. Perhaps we can see the way the early Church changed the promise in the way Paul tells the Corinthians "Do you not know that the saints will judge the world?" (1 Cor. 6.2). These passages in Matthew and Luke therefore explain to the disciples their role at the judgement. The disciples were so certain of their roles in the kingdom that they argued about who would take precedence (Matt. 18.1–5, par.) and the mother of James and John asked that her sons be given positions of power (Matt. 20.20–28, par.). Once we understand that often the teaching of Jesus about forgiveness was originally used by Jesus to train the twelve disciples for their roles as "judges," a number of problems with these texts are resolved.

Our first difficulty is to know why Jesus continued to associate with people who were wicked and not demand that they repent. It was this behavior that gave such offence to the Pharisees. Why did Jesus not demand that these "sinners" repent, offer sacrifice and make restitution? There is only one passage in the gospels in which Jesus follows the demands of the Law. It is the passage where Jesus tells the cleansed leper to show himself to a priest and make an offering (Mk. 1.44, par.). It may be that Mark has told this story in just this way to parallel the story of healing performed by Elisha (2 Kings 5.1–14). In both stories the leper is sent off to perform a special task. A similar relationship can be seen in the telling of the raising of a dead child (2 Kings 4.32–37, Mk. 5.21–43, par.). If Jesus followed society's rule for lepers, why no mention of him following the rule and requiring repentance, restitution and sacrifice. We learn from the call of Levi (Mk. 2.13–17, par.) that Jesus had a tax collector among his group. He was one of the "many tax collectors and sinners" (Mk. 2.15) that ate with Jesus that night. We are not told that Levi repented, made restitution, offered sacrifice, we are told that he "followed" Jesus. Even Zacchaeus was not required to make restitution or offer sacrifice (Lk. 19.1–10). Indeed we are told that Jesus, teaching in the temple, said that "tax collectors and harlots" would go into the kingdom of God before the chief priest and elders of the people (Matt. 21.23–32). The next passage and Matthew 11.18f makes it clear that John's message differed from that of Jesus on the question of repentance. John seems to have been a preacher of repentance and righteousness, whereas Jesus, the friend of sinners, proclaimed God's acceptance of sinners. Jesus associated with the wicked of Israel, not making his friendship dependent on their conversion to the law, because he saw his action as a sign that God would soon save them. He also continued to associate with these people because it was an important part of his training of the twelve. It was important that they know and understand the people they would judge at the final day. People were offended because he continued to associate with these people. Jesus taught the disciples that "those who are well have no need of a physician, but those who are sick; I came not to call the righteous, but sinners" (Mk. 2.17, par.). In this way Jesus trained the disciples in the cure of souls.

Sanders proposes that "the novelty and offence of Jesus' message was that the wicked who heeded him would be included in the kingdom even though they did not repent as was universally understood—that is, even though they did not make restitution, sacrifice and turn to obedience to the law."[142] He finds that the teachings of Perrin, Jeremias, Käsemann, Riches, Fuchs, Behm, Funk, and Westerholm are in general agreement in saying that Jesus was killed because he offered sinners forgiveness. Sanders considers that that view places an unfair interpretation on Jewish teaching of the time. The leaders of Judaism would have welcomed the conversion of "sinners and tax collectors." The point is that Jesus was seen to be a friend of those who continued to be sinners.

Sanders speculative proposal, however, with its implication that Jesus claimed to know whom God would include and not include in the kingdom and the implication of a downgrading of the "normal machinery of righteousness, would push Jesus' stance close to, or over, the border which sepa.ated individual charisma from impiety."[143] Our suggestion, however, that Jesus associated with "publicans and sinners" so that he could train the twelve answers the problems raised by Sanders in this section of his book.

Another question raised by Sanders is why Jesus taught the twelve about judgement without, so the weight of the evidence suggests, speaking of an impending judgement and subsequent restoration of Israel? Sanders lists various indications of restoration eschatology in the teaching of Jesus. He finds that the sayings about the rebuilding of the temple (Mk. 11.15–19, par., Mk. 13.2, par., Mk. 14.58, par.), and the sayings about Israel and the twelve (Matt. 10.6, 19.28) most important. When he comes to consider the judgement he finds that the theme of many of the biblical prophets who speak of Israel as a nation awaiting a judgement from which only a remnant will survive receives little emphasis in the teaching of Jesus. Bultmann makes the same point in his *Theology of the New Testament.* In the preaching of Jesus "The judgement is coming not on nations but on individuals who must give an account of themselves before God; and it is individuals whom coming salvation will bless."[144] Sanders agrees that the themes of national repentance, forgiveness and judgement are absent from the sayings of Jesus. Yet he holds that this does not prove that Jesus opposed Jewish nationalism. He feels that there are "clear and undeniable indications that he expected the restoration of Israel, temple and twelve are national symbols. ... What is surprising is that, while looking for the restoration of Israel, he did not follow the majority and urge the traditional means towards that end: repentance and a return to the observance of the law."[145]

We can now understand why Jesus spoke to his disciples about judgement without speaking of the impending judgement of the nation or predicting the restoration of Israel. Many of the passages that have Jesus call for national repentance do not seem to be authentic. Some seem designed to make the message of Jesus conform to John's message (Mk. 1.15f). The praise of the gentiles and the condemnation of Israel in other passages seem to be the hand of the early Church (Matt. 11.21–24, 12.41f). The more authentic teaching of Jesus implies an individual judgement (Matt. 13.24–30, 13.47–50). Jesus promised that "it is better for you to enter the kingdom of God with one eye than with two eyes be thrown into hell" (Mk. 9.47, par.). The parables of judgement, the parable of the Wheat and the Tares (Matt. 13.24–30, par.) and the parable of the Dragnet (Matt. 13.47–50) also speak of individual selection.

Jesus seems to have looked forward to the restoration of Israel (Mk. 9.12, Matt. 17.11, Acts 1.6), but it was not his task to preach a call for national repentance that would lead to Jewish restoration. His task was to prepare those disciples who would sit in judgement. Individual selection would be their duty on that "last day."

We can now understand why Jesus was not a preacher of repentance. Almost all the texts that tell of Jesus teaching repentance are peculiar to Luke. They are the parables of the Pharisee and the Tax Collector (Lk. 18.9–14), the story of Zacchaeus (Lk. 19.1–10) and the comments added to the parables of the Lost Sheep and the Lost Coin (Lk. 15.7, 10). There are other passages that read as though they were added because the evangelists thought that Jesus must have taught repentance (Mk. 1.14f, par., 6.12, par.). These passages may well be the work of a Church that did not feel as close to unrepentant sinners as Jesus seems to have been.

Finally, what training did Jesus give his disciples about the inclusion of the gentiles? In the Old Testament there are passages that suggest that, at the last day, the gentiles will be included in God's salvation (Isa. 49.6, Micah 4.5f) and at the other extreme there are passages that speak of the enslavement (Isa. 45.14, 49.23) and of the destruction of the gentiles (Isa. 54.3). So in the gospels, it is difficult to reconcile passages that speak of a gentile mission (Matt. 8.11f, par., 10.18, Mk. 13.10, par., 14.9) with those that suggest that Jesus limited his activity to Israel (Matt. 10.5, 15.21–28). Both this last passage and Matthew 8.5–13 tell of Jesus healing gentiles yet he keeps his distance. Jesus seems to have little to do with the gentiles yet after the resurrection his disciples soon began a gentile mission. We can best understand the debate in early Christianity that is mentioned in Galatians if we agree that Jesus accepted what would seem to be the majority Jewish opinion that the gentiles, or some at least of the gentiles, would be admitted to the kingdom. His cleaning of the court of the gentiles (Mk. 11.15–19, par.) and the saying "My house shall be a house of prayer for all the nations" (11.17) probably reflects his attitude. Yet it was not his task to preach the message of God to the gentiles. His task was to prepare for that kingdom by training the twelve.

The reports of Jesus eating with "publicans and sinners" have been mentioned in this chapter. We turn now to other meals that Jesus had with the twelve that had such an important place in their life together.

8. Eating Together

The meals that Jesus shared with his disciples, including those in the company of "publicans and sinners," came to mean much more than sustenance. These meals can be seen as "training sessions" for the twelve. There were also meals of feasting and rejoicing. The marriage in Cana is an example (Jn. 2.1–11). Jesus was accused of coming "eating and drinking, and they say, 'Behold, a glutton and a drunkard'" (Matt. 11.19, par.). Then there were meals that Jesus held with his disciples at homes of those who supported his ministry (Mk. 1.29–31, par., Lk. 10.38f). There were private meals that Jesus had with his disciples, the most important of these was the "last supper" held just before the crucifixion. There were meals that looked forward to the "messianic banquet" when "many will come from east and west and sit at table with Abraham, Isaac and Jacob in the kingdom of heaven" (Matt. 8.11).

We can begin our study of the background of these meals of Jesus with the disaster that came to Adam and Eve when they ate together and rejected God's command (Gen. 3.1–7). From that time on scripture sees almost every meal mentioned as having a religious aspect. All food was seen as a gift from God. Therefore there was a tithe on all animal and vegetable produce (Num. 18). When this tithe and other offerings and sacrifices are brought "you shall eat before the Lord your God, and you shall rejoice" (Deut. 12.7). When Jethro met the children of Israel in the wilderness he offered sacrifice and "Aaron came with all the elders of Israel to eat bread with Moses' father-in-law before God" (Ex. 18.12). The reconciliation between Jacob and Laban was an occasion for a sacrifice and a meal "and Jacob offered a sacrifice on the mountain and called his kinsmen to eat bread; and they ate bread and tarried all night on the mountain" (Gen. 31.54). This connection between a sacrifice and sharing a meal was quite common. There was no thought that Yahweh ate the portion of the animal that was offered on the altar, nor was there any suggestion that the worshippers ate the deity. These were pagan notions condemned by the prophets (Jer. 44.19f). God perhaps "smelled the sweet savor" and was seen as sharing in the rejoicing over the meal (1 Sam. 9.11f, Prov. 9.1–6). When Moses and the elders went up the mountain and saw God without being harmed "he did not lay his hand on the chief men of the people of Israel, they beheld God, and ate and drank" (Ex. 24.11). All meals, therefore, whether they were part of a formal sacrifice offered at the temple or only an informal family meal, had a religious aspect. They were always a time of sharing between God and man.

In the later books of the Old Testament, meals became part of the messianic promise. People came to look forward to the day when they would join in a great feast with the Messiah in the kingdom. Ezekiel tells of a day when God will seek all the scattered sheep of Israel "And I will bring them out from the peoples, and gather them from the countries; and will bring them into their own land; and I will feed them on the mountains of Israel" (Ezek. 34.13). Zechariah tells us how good that day will be, "Yea, how good and fair it shall be. Grain shall make the young men flourish, and new wine the maidens" (Zec. 9.17). Isaiah tells us that it will be a great feast "a feast of fat things, a feast of wine on the lees, of fat things full of marrow" (Isa. 25.6). There are similar promises in Isaiah 55.2 and 65.13. This image grew more intense during the intertestamental period. We can see something of the importance of the promise in 4 Ezra 8.52–54 and 2 Baruch 29.8.

Jesus looked forward to this day of feasting in the kingdom. He spoke of those who would come "from east and west and from north and south and sit at table in the kingdom of God" (Lk. 13.29, Matt. 8.11). Several parables tell us that the kingdom is like a banquet to which many are called (Lk. 12.37f, Matt. 25.1f). Before his death Jesus looked forward to drinking the fruit of the vine in the kingdom of God" (Mk. 14.25, par.). Yet the meals of Jesus were more than a foretaste of the messianic meal. They had an important role in the preparation of the twelve.

When Norman Perrin set out to rediscover the original teaching of Jesus, he called this table-fellowship with the disciples and "tax collectors and sinners" an acted parable. Yet it is more than an acted parable; "it is the aspect of Jesus' ministry which must have been most meaningful to his followers and most offensive to his critics."[146] Perrin suggests that the communal meals of the earliest Christianity must be seen as evidence for this practice of Jesus. A study of the book of Acts, the Epistles and the Didache will show that these meals were very important. Perrin argues that because there is a great variety in the theological purpose of the meals, "The practice of the early Christian communal meals existed before there was a specifically Christian theology to give it meaning."[147] After rejecting the suggestion that this early Christian practice came from the last supper, or from Jewish or Qumran meals, he concludes that the early Christian communal meals "are a continuation of the regular practice of the ministry of Jesus."[148] This conclusion is supported by the work of E. Lohmeyer in his book *Lord of the Temple* where he discusses the central role of table-fellowship in the ministry of Jesus.[149]

According to Perrin, there are two sayings, "indubitably authentic," that are of great significance in this context. The first is Matthew 11.16–19, par., especially "Behold, a glutton and a drunkard, a friend of tax collectors and sinners" (verse 19). Perrin suggests that this passage tells us that it was the practice of Jesus to hold joyous table-fellowship with tax collectors and other Jews who made themselves as gentiles.

The second passage is Matthew 8.11, par. "I tell you, many will come from the east and west and sit at table with Abraham, Isaac and Jacob in the kingdom of heaven." Perrin tells us that this passage demands a setting of table-fellowship. It refers to the expected messianic banquet and emphasizes its universalism. It tells us that table-fellowship in the ministry of Jesus may be seen as an anticipation of table-fellowship in "the kingdom."

From this study of these passages and his previous study of parables that tell of Jesus' relationship to "tax collectors and sinners," such as the Prodigal Son, the Lost Sheep and the Lost Coin, Perrin concludes that a feature of the common life of Jesus was the way "Scribe, tax collector, fisherman and Zealot came together around the table at which they celebrated the joy of the present experience and anticipated its consummation in the future."[150] He goes on to suggest that it was the memory of this fellowship that led to the development of the eucharistic fellowship of the early Church.

It is difficult to accept this suggestion. It must have been something more than just the memory of things past that resulted in "a table-fellowship of such joy and gladness that it survived the crucifixion and provided the focal point for the community life of the early Christians."[151] Tax collectors and sinners were not included in the table-fellowship of the early Church.

We can, however, agree with Perrin that we must see this table-fellowship of Jesus as a central feature of his ministry. It was part of his anticipation of the end-time. The meals provided the setting for much of the private teaching the disciples received from Jesus.

Perrin ends his discussion of these meals by saying that "the disciples must have come to know the special way that Jesus had of 'breaking bread' which gave rise to the legend of the Emmaus road" (Lk.

24.35).[152] We again can accept this statement if we were to change "gave rise to the legend" to "help us to understand what happened at Em-maus."

From the reports that we have in the New Testament of Jesus eating with his disciples, it is impossible to be certain if any of the more formal Jewish religious meals of the time can provide a pattern for his gatherings.[153] Meals must have formed a focus for the enjoyment of fellowship. This seems implied by the passage about fasting (Mk. 2.18–20, par.). We have a more ordinary domestic scene in a passage peculiar to Luke that tells of Martha preparing a meal while Mary sat at Jesus' feet (Lk. 10.38f). In other passages common to all three synoptics there is a particular relationship between the meals and discipleship. After the call of Peter and John we are told that the group went to Peter's home and after the mother of Peter's wife was healed, they ate together (Mk. 1.29, 30, par.). Again, after the call of Levi there was a meal at his home and "as he sat at table in his house many tax collectors and sinners were sitting with Jesus and his disciples for there were many who followed him" (Mk. 2.15, par.). In Mark's gospel we have the strange passage that tells of the attempt by family and friends to take control of Jesus because they thought he was mad. The passage is of interest because it is placed by Mark just after the call of the twelve and again we have the mention of a group gathered for a meal (Mk. 3.20).

It is Mark again who makes the connection between the disciples and eating after the disciples return from their preaching mission (Mk. 6.30f). Jesus says to them "Come away by yourselves to a lonely place and rest awhile, for many were coming and going and they had no leisure even to eat" (Mk. 6.31). They then go by boat to a deserted place. When the disciples come, toward the end of the day, to suggest that Jesus send the crowds that have followed to the neighboring villages for food, Jesus suggests that the disciples feed them themselves. The language that is used to describe the taking of the five loaves and two fishes, the breaking of bread, the blessing and distribution, is very like the language used to describe similar actions at the last supper. This pattern is repeated in the report of the feeding of the four thousand (Mk. 8.1f, par.). We have another example of the openness of the meals of Jesus in Mark 7.1–4 and parallel. In Mark's version the Pharisees and scribes from Jerusalem see the disciples eat without the customary ritual washing. Luke has a Pharisee invite Jesus and the disciples to dinner and then comment on the disciples' manner. The pattern of Jesus' meals, at least in this respect, was not in accordance with Pharisaic teaching.

Many people seem to have sought out Jesus so that they could eat with him and his disciples (Matt.9.10, Mk. 2.15, Lk. 5.29, 7.36f). When the Syrophoenician woman called on him to cure her daughter Jesus tells her "it is not right to take the children's bread and throw it to dogs" (Mk. 7.24–30, par.). Eating with the disciples and with the children of Israel, especially with the "lost sheep" of the house of Israel, would seem to have been of great importance to Jesus.

In John's gospel, there are far fewer references to Jesus eating with his disciples. The gospel begins the public ministry of Jesus with a wedding party. We again have the pattern of the call of the disciples and a gathering at which Jesus eats with the disciples. In John's own way his report of the wedding feast at Cana may be his summary of the tradition that Jesus ate regularly in a special festive way with his disciples. The reference to the joy while the bridegroom is present may be an echo of the synoptics. John also reports on the feeding in the wilderness (Jn. 6.1–14) and follows it with his teaching on the eucharist "and the bread which I shall give for the life of the world is my flesh" (Jn. 6.51). This passage and two others that mention eating are tied to a religious feast at Jerusalem (Jn. 7.37f, 13.2f).

We cannot establish the pattern of the meals that Jesus had with disciples, but we may be able to identify one important element of those meals. We are told in the Acts of the Apostles that the early Christians met for the "breaking of bread." Acts 2.42 tells us "And they devoted themselves to the apostles' teaching and fellowship, to the breaking of bread and the prayers." Then in the next paragraph, "And day by day, attending the temple together and breaking bread in their homes, they partook of food with glad and generous hearts" (Acts 2.46). In another passage in Acts telling of Paul's missionary travels, the eucharistic meal is spoken of simply as a "breaking of bread" (Acts 20.7f). There is an obvious connection between this practice and the meals of Jesus. For those early Christians the promise of Jesus that "where two or three are gathered in my name, there am I in the midst of them" (Matt. 18.20) was very real. At the last supper we are told that "as they were eating, he took bread, and blessed, and broke it, and gave it to them" (Mk. 14.22, par.). At the feeding of the five thousand and then at the feeding of the four thousand "he looked up to heaven and blessed and broke the loaves and gave them to the disciples" (Mk. 6.41, par.). Again,

on the walk to Emmaus, when they stopped for the evening, "he took
the bread and blessed and broke it, and gave it to them" (Lk. 24.30).
Apparently, in the early Church, the essential element in the eucharist
was bread. There is no mention of wine in these texts except at the last
supper.

Oscar Cullmann in an essay entitled *The Meaning of the Lord's Supper in Primitive Christianity* examines other early Christian texts concerning the eucharistic meal.[154] Again we find cultic meals in which the
essential element was bread. For instance there is a eucharistic meal
mentioned in the Acts of John (106–10) and in the Acts of Thomas
(27.49, 50, 133), in which there is no mention of wine. There are
times when another element is added to the bread but it is not necessarily wine and not always a drink. Until the third century, certain districts
used water instead of wine (Acts of Thomas 120f, Acts of Peter). In
Judaic Christianity, if we accept the traditions preserved in Pseudo-
Clementine, the Lord's Supper was celebrated with bread and salt
(Hom. Diamartyria IV, and Hom. XIV. 7). We also need to remember
that a drink of milk and honey was given to the newly baptized at their
first eucharist in the early Church[155] and that early Christian art frequently represents the eucharist under the form of a meal of loaves and
fishes. One can see such an early Christian mosaic on the shores of
Galilee today.[156]

We suggested, in Chapter 2, that Jesus and his close disciples realized that they faced martyrdom or at least the possibility of martyrdom.
Jesus called on them to take up their cross and follow him. We have
seen that this can be understood to mean that they must, like Isaac, be
prepared to face death. Luke adds to the Cross sayings the word
"daily" (Lk. 9.23). This addition can be seen as an attempt to spiritualize the saying and make it apply to all Christians, not just to the twelve.
Yet there may have been a daily reminder that as the group went toward
Jerusalem, it went toward death. That reminder may have been made at
the meals that Jesus had "daily" with his disciples.

We must consider the expression "the breaking of bread" a strange
way to speak about a meal. The emphasis is completely on the breaking
of the bread and not on the eating of the bread. We would normally
speak about "eating bread" if that was the meal. There must have been
something very special about the way Jesus "broke" bread for the expression to have become so important. It is always Jesus who "breaks"
the bread, at Emmaus, at the miraculous feedings, at the last supper. It
is difficult to understand how the "breaking of bread" could so quickly

have come to have such an important place in the early Church if these were the only occasions it was mentioned and the last supper the only occasion on which the implications of the action was made clear. We must remember also that, in John's teaching on the eucharist in Chapter 6 of his gospel, Jesus speaks of the "the bread which I shall give for the life of the world is my flesh" (Jn. 6.51). Again, we have the connection between bread being distributed by Jesus and a prophecy of a death soon to come.

The connection between "breaking" and death is very clear in another passage from John's gospel. At one time it was thought that the passage that tells of the "breaking of legs" in John 19.31–34 was likely an invention of that gospel writer. We know that the Romans used crucifixion as a means of execution of slaves and foreign rebels. In 71 BC, six thousand slaves involved in the Spartacus uprising were crucified and left to hang on poles placed the length of the Appian Way. The suggestion that the two crucified with Jesus had their legs broken to hasten their death and that when they came to break the legs of Jesus he was found to have already died was thought by many to be written so that John might show that Jesus was the Paschal lamb. Exodus 12.46 requires that "you shall not break a bone of it." There is also a messianic prophecy in Psalm 34.20 "He keeps all his bones, not one of them is broken." At the 1968 Giv'at ha-Mivtar excavations an adult skeleton showed that the victim had died from crucifixion.[157] The broken legs provide the most explicit corroboration of John's information that it was the practice for Jewish crucifixion victims to have their legs broken. This would hasten death as, without support from the legs, the victim would no longer be able to breath. It may well be that this procedure was carried out on Jewish victims because it was against the Mosaic law to leave a body on its cross overnight. If this was standard procedure for crucifixion in Israel at the time, Jesus may well have expected to have his body broken when he came to die.

If Jesus did spend much of his time training the twelve, it would be strange if their meals, that had such a significant place in their ministry, did not have a special feature that set them apart. If we picture Jesus taking bread, as he did at the last of those suppers, as he did at the miraculous feedings, and breaking that bread apart, we have an image that would have been imprinted on the minds of the disciples.

Our suggestion then is that during his ministry Jesus took bread and broke it and gave it to his small group of disciples as a sign of what was to come in the future. There are two other passages we should consider.

On a boat journey the disciples had forgotten to bring enough bread (Mk. 8.14–21, Matt. 16.5–12). Mark tells us that "they had only one loaf in the boat" (Mk.8.14). Jesus then speaks to the disciples about "the leaven of the Pharisees" (Mk. 8.15). If we remove this passage as an interpolation, (it is found separately in Lk. 12.1, 2) we have a straightforward passage that speaks of the breaking of bread on two occasions. The disciples are told that what bread they have will be enough for what really matters, the evening breaking of bread together. They need the bread not for food but to share. Jesus asks them "Do you not remember when I broke five loaves for the five thousand" (Mk. 8.18, 19).

The other passage we should consider is the discussion in John Chapter 6 about Jesus as the bread of life. The "Jews" dispute saying "How can this man give us his flesh to eat?" (Jn. 6.52). Jesus replies with the saying, "Truly, truly, I say to you, unless you eat the flesh of the Son of Man and drink his blood, you have no life in you" (Jn. 6.53). J.C. O'Neill points out, "This saying has the highest claims to be taken as an authentic word of Jesus, since it begins, 'Amen'; since it contains the expression 'Son of Man' which the early Church used rarely, if at all; and since it occurs in another version outside the canon, in the Naassene Gospel."[158] In Jewish thinking the term "flesh and blood" is used in reference to sacrifice.[159] In speaking of eating his flesh and blood, Jesus is saying, in the rest of this passage, that true life will come through his sacrificial death, that "he who eats with me will live because of me" (Jn. 6.57) indeed, "he who eats this bread will live forever" (Jn. 6.58). In the resurrection appearances, therefore, John reports that Jesus showed the disciples his body (Jn. 20.20, 27).

We conclude that Jesus, at his meals with the disciples, on other occasions with "publicans and sinners," and at the feeding of the five thousand, took bread, blessed it, broke it and gave it to all that had gathered. These actions came to be a reminder in the midst of the rejoicing of what the future could bring. A reminder to the disciples that they must daily bear their own cross. This would explain why "the breaking of bread" so quickly became the Christian way of worship. This would explain why bread alone was the essential element in the worship of the early Church. It would explain why the *Agape* meal had such importance in the early Church (Jude 12). It would also explain the importance of the meals the gospel writers tell us about that took place at the resurrection. It would explain why the book of Acts, in several places mentions Jesus eating with his disciples.

9. Conclusion

In the past we have tended to picture Jesus as a solitary, wandering preacher, his message addressed to the great crowds that gathered wherever he travelled. The sermons he preached with their wonderful illustrations and parables, the healings and exorcisms he performed, brought a great response throughout Israel.

Our study has shown that there is reason to question every one of these assumptions. Jesus was not a solitary. Each gospel makes that point. He appears to have been very gregarious. He enjoyed a party. At the beginning of his ministry Jesus gathered a special group "to be with him." Other groups seem to have followed him to Jerusalem, "the women," and the "brethren of the Lord," but the only group that we have any real knowledge about is the twelve.

We also found that Jesus was not a wanderer. His ministry was largely located in a small area of Galilee, probably centered about Capernaum. By some, Jesus was called "Rabbi" and "teacher." In Judaism such a person was usually identified with a local, stable life. We also found that most of his time was spent in training his small group of disciples. The famous "Sermon on the Mount" and his parables must be understood as being addressed primarily to the twelve. The healing miracles, the signs of the kingdom, were used in the training of the twelve. Jesus taught them to share in his knowledge of "the Father" in a life of prayer. The forgiveness proclaimed must be seen as training for the ingathering of the twelve tribes of Israel, soon to be judged by the twelve. The "cross-bearing" that the disciples were called to share was no spiritualized burden-bearing but a call to face the literal possibility of martyrdom.

We suggested that the disciples were reminded of the possibility of martyrdom every evening when Jesus at supper, took the bread, and blessed it, and broke it, and gave it to them. The meals that Jesus shared with the disciples and others were an important part of the ministry.

Almost every part of the gospel story that we have seen as addressed to the "crowds that followed him" and indirectly to the people of the early Church, must be seen as having been addressed to the twelve.

Part Four

Eating with the Lord

With a small group, leadership is all important. When the leadership is removed the small group disintegrates. The small group that centered about Jesus, who ate together, slept together, travelled together, had committed their lives to martyrdom and discipleship. To that end they had trained as healers and exorcists, as men of prayer who learned to live constantly in the presence of God. They had studied the scriptures and had learned to understand parables and signs. They had come to accept God's love and forgiveness and had trained to be "judges" of the "kingdom." Yet, when the crucifixion came they "all forsook him and fled" (Mk. 14.50).

How was the small group that Jesus had established re-formed? The history of the Christian Church shows that Jesus' small group of disciples was reestablished and that it then proceeded to "turn the world upside down" (Acts 17.6). It is difficult to understand the re-formation of the group if nothing actually happened in the historical life of Jesus. There are those who are hostile to the very idea of the miraculous. They see the resurrection as a gradual development of a faith or trust in Jesus. That "existential" experience came to be explained in "resurrection" language. Such an explanation or understanding does have the advantage of accounting for the discrepancies in the various accounts of the resurrection. Advocates of this view suggest that the resurrection accounts are not to be seen as history, but as reports of the emotional experience of the believers. Some accounts can be explained as apologetic material developed by the early Church. The account of the guard at the tomb in Matthew is an example. Another way of looking at the accounts is to see them as a kind of recapitulation of the gospel writers' main themes.

If we see the Easter narratives as expressions of faith rather than as the historical evidence that is the basis of faith, we are immediately faced with the difficulty that Paul, in 1 Corinthians 15, refers his readers to a list of appearances that are obviously seen to be the basis of faith. Certainly Paul thought that his own experience of the resurrected Jesus was important. He also tells us that the rather formal, stylized formula that listed some appearances had been handed down and carefully preserved by the infant Church. The crucifixion, burial and resurrection "on the third day" and then the appearances of Jesus all have theological meaning for Paul. These closely connected parts of the "life" of Jesus are often recalled, although he seems to have been otherwise uninterested in the historical Jesus.

The word *opthe* used by Paul in 1 Corinthians 15 suggests a vision. Yet the language that Paul uses accentuates the revelatory action of Jesus. There is no emphasis on the emotional experience of the recipient. Those who suggest that the contemplation of the meaning of the death of Jesus and the emotional stress involved led to a series of "visions" must explain the great diversity in the accounts we have received and the complete absence of any suggestion that what happened was "just" a vision. They must also explain how a series of visions led the disciples to a belief in the personal resurrection of Jesus. Could such a series of revelations in the individual lives of the disciples lead to the resurrection faith of the Church? Or is it more likely that some event in the life of Jesus lead to the belief of the disciples? It is difficult to arrive at any other explanation. Living communication with Jesus continued after his death and led to the re-formation of the small group he had gathered about him.

Thus the empty tomb is a necessary condition of any claim about the continuing presence and activity of Jesus. It cannot be seen as verification of the resurrection, but given the biblical understanding of personality it is difficult to imagine how one could separate the continuing presence and activity of the crucified Jesus from the resurrection of the body. In a sense the resurrection is already presupposed in the telling of the story. Rather than see the empty tomb as a symbol and myth devised by a believing Church, it is best to see behind the narrative historical fact, the reminiscences of those involved. The reports may have been confused and distorted, but they provide valid reasons for believing that the tomb was found empty. Except for the emendations and additions in Matthew, there is little in the gospels that can be called apologetic. Indeed, if the story were legend, created for this purpose, it is hard to understand why the only witnesses in Mark 16 were women who by Jewish law were incompetent to testify. There are also difficulties with the appearance stories. They do not read as eyewitness reports, yet they cannot be reduced to mythological creations. There is very little emphasis on the supernatural. Almost all the emphasis is on the humanity of Jesus.

If we agree that "something" had to happen to evoke the faith of the disciples, we believe that we can show that the "something" was the "real presence" of Jesus with his disciples at meals. In this way the pattern of life he had established with his small group continued.

That "something" probably took place in Galilee and at Jerusalem. The earliest tradition of the Easter events, 1 Corinthians 15 does not give a location for the appearances. Paul probably received this tradition from the Hellenistic community at Damascus. It had been part of his Christian education, "I delivered to you as of first importance what I also received" (1 Cor. 15.3). That Christian community probably received it from the earliest Aramaic speaking Church in Palestine. We tend to accept the tradition as though it were all of one piece, with each appearance taking place in sequence. Certainly Paul's repeated use of the word "then" gives that impression. Yet, it is obvious that Paul did not "receive" from others the report about an appearance to himself. The same is true with the comment that tells us that the majority of the five hundred were still alive when Paul wrote the passage (1. Cor. 15.6). These passages must have been written by Paul. Verses 3 and 4 (1 Cor. 15), read like a summary of the faith, both verses are marked by the Greek phrase *kata tas graphas,* according to the scriptures. To this short creed Paul perhaps added two traditional lists of resurrection appearances. The parallelism between the two lists is made clear by Paul's use of language, "he appeared to Cephas, then to the twelve... he appeared to James, then to all the apostles." To these lists Paul adds the appearances that grew out of the mission of each group. To Cephas and the twelve, Paul adds the appearance to the five hundred. To the appearance to James and the apostles, Paul adds the appearance to himself. He is able in this way to join the two lists of appearances, the one, we suggest, having grown out of the experiences of the twelve in

Galilee, the other out of the experiences of the women and the brethren in Jerusalem.

Peter and James both came to leadership positions in the early Church. We can tell something about their relationship in Galatians 2.9, 10. Lists of appearances that developed about the same time at separate locations would be remembered separately until they were put together in some sort of order. Whether it was Paul who united these two lists or they were already joined in the tradition he received we cannot tell. The careful use of chronological adverbs is intended to create the impression that the appearances occurred in succession. That impression is reinforced by the way Paul adds the appearances to himself as "last of all" (1 Cor. 15.8).

The reasons for believing that the first meeting that the disciples had with the risen Christ took place in Galilee are very strong. It is expressly stated by Mark twice, 14.28 and 16.7. Matthew follows Mark in Matthew 28.16, whereas John's gospel is oriented to Jerusalem and the supplementary chapter is set in Galilee. Only Luke sets all the events of Easter in Jerusalem and this is probably because of his theological plan. The appearance to the five hundred that Paul mentions is more likely set in Galilee than in Jerusalem. It would be a large gathering for such a hostile city.

Let us now attempt to trace the pattern of appearances in Jerusalem and Galilee.

1. The Events at the Tomb

Paul, in 1 Corinthians 15, does not mention the visit of the women to the tomb. Some have suggested that the resurrection is not, therefore, to be understood literally but emotionally.

If the resurrection is to be understood as a "spiritual" event in the lives of the disciples and not as an event in the life of Jesus, it is difficult to explain why, from the earliest times, one day came to be called the "Lord's Day." The early Church was certain that it was on this day that Christ rose from the dead. In the very beginning it was simply called the first day of the week (Mk. 16.2), following the Jewish system of dating. The gospel accounts of the events that began when the women first came to the tomb are dated this way. Paul uses the phrase in 1 Corinthians 16.2 when he calls on the Corinthians to take a special collection on that day. Acts 20.4–15 tells of Paul's sermon at Troas when the Christians gathered for worship on "the first day of the week." The first use of the expression "the Lord's Day" is in Revelation 1.10. This became the normal designation of the day of Christian worship in the later literature.[160]

Another difficulty is to explain how the phrase "on the third day" came to be such an important part of the *kerygma* of the primitive Church. Some appear willing to accept almost any explanation so long as it does not claim that something very special took place "on the third day." The expression is used in Jewish literature to suggest that God never leaves the just in danger for more than three days. Yet most of this rabbinic literature is quite late. The passage "in accordance with the scripture" in 1 Corinthians 15.3 has led some to suggest a doctrinal rather than an historical original for the phrase. The obvious text that could be used in this way is Hosea 6.2 "After two days he will revive us, on the third day he will raise us up." Yet if this passage is the source of the phrase "on the third day" it is strange that the passage from Hosea does not appear on the lists of proof texts used by the early Church.[161]

There have been numerous other suggestions from the History of Religion School and from Jewish speculation about the end of time.[162] The large number of suggestions and their complexity lead one to believe that it is very difficult to deny the events at the tomb "on the third day."

We have suggested in our section on "Cross-bearing" that Jesus himself may have unknowingly prepared the way for these events by using the expression to say that he believed that God, the Father would care for him even in death and that in a very short time he would be saved. He may have mentioned the "sign" of Jonah at this time and therefore those "Q" passages (Matt. 12.39–41, 16.4, par.) may well be based on an authentic reference of Jesus.

The empty tomb itself is another difficulty for those who would deny the reality of the resurrection. If those who opposed Christianity could have pointed to his tomb, preaching would have been stifled. Even the suggestion that his body had been disposed of by the authorities, as was the normal procedure for criminals, was denied by the fact of the empty tomb and the burial by Nicodemus. The story of the guard at the tomb in Matthew shows that these accusations could not be made by his enemies. The accusation made was that the disciples stole his body (Matt. 27.62). However, the word Paul uses in 1 Corinthians 15.4 that we translate "was raised" implies that he knew the tomb was empty. He

would probably have used another word if he had been uncertain.[163] He
appears to have accepted the usual Jewish hope of resurrection as he explains in Romans 8.11 "he who raised Jesus Christ from the dead will
give life to your mortal bodies."

Another accusation that must have been made was that Jesus had
been buried in a plain linen cloth, unanointed, like a common criminal.
Jewish opponents must have seized on this as an additional sign of dis-
grace. The reply made by the early Church was that Jesus had been
anointed.

There are four accounts of the anointing of Jesus, one in each of the
gospels (Mk. 14.3–9, Matt. 26.6–13, Lk. 7.36–50, Jn. 12.3–8).
There are significant differences among these four accounts in the time,
and place, and manner of the anointing. Each evangelist seems to have
used the incident for his own theological purpose. Yet there are also
striking similarities that makes it likely that all four accounts relate to
one incident in the life of Jesus. In all four accounts a woman anoints
Jesus, causing objections which Jesus quashes by approving of the
woman's act.

The less complicated version of the incident is in Luke. He knows
nothing of an anointing by Joseph and Nicodemus and he has the
women come to the tomb too late. Nor is there any allusion to the death
of Jesus in the incident, placed outside the passion narrative, in which a
sinful woman comes to Jesus washes his feet with her tears and dries his
feet with her hair.

This story now set at Bethany is used by Mark to begin his passion
narrative. A story of a simple washing becomes a proleptic anointing of
Jesus for his burial (Mk. 14.8) "She has done what she could, she had
anointed my body beforehand for burying." We are meant to infer,
from the ointment being poured on the head of Jesus, that it covered his
body. In the argument that follows Jesus makes the point that she has
done a "good work," which should be understood in the rabbinic sense
of the words which includes almsgivings, welcoming strangers, visiting
the sick, burying the dead. The "good work" she has done, Jesus
argues, falls in this last category. The incident is placed after the entry
into Jerusalem and very near the Passover. Mark continues this theme as
he gives his reason for the visit of the women to the tomb. He tells us
that "when the sabbath was past" the women "bought spices, so that
they might go and anoint him" (Mk. 16.1). Aside from the problem of
shopping "very early on the first day of the week" it is difficult to believe that the women came to the tomb, in a rather warm climate, to

anoint a body, after three days. One of the literary characteristics of
Mark is that he frames sections of his gospel by related stories. His two
feeding stories frame one section (Mk. 6.30–44, 8.1–9) the two stories
of the giving of sight another (Mk. 8.22–26, 10.46–52). The passion
narrative is framed by two anointing stories, the one calls attention to
the other.

Mark is very hard on the disciples. In our chapter on healing we
pointed out that each section of his gospel ends with a comment on their
blindness. The progressive character of the healing in Mark 8.22f can
be seen as a commentary on the gradual opening of the eyes of the disciples, the second healing of a blind man as commentary on the failure of
Peter to see (Mk. 10.46f). The passion story ends with the promise that
the disciples will finally "see" Jesus in Galilee. One disciple betrays
him, another denies him, and they all fail him (Mk. 14.50). At the end it
is the centurion and not one of the disciples that says "Truly, this man
was the Son of God" (Mk. 15.39).

The women disciples watch all this from afar but they also fail to understand. They come to the tomb "on the first day of the week" to complete a burial. We are forced to contrast their lack of understanding with
the women who came unannounced to the house of Simon the leper to
anoint his body (Mk. 14.3f). Verse nine tells us that "wherever the gospel is preached in the whole world, what she had done will be told in
memory of her." This is Mark's way of saying that this unknown
woman is much more important than any of the well-known women disciples. We can only speculate why Mark took this attitude to the disciples but it does help us understand why he ended his gospel with the
words "they went out and fled the tomb; for trembling and astonishment had come on them and they had said nothing to any one, for they
were afraid" (Mk. 16.8). They were just like the male disciples who,
when they began to understand what they had to face, "were amazed,
and those that followed were afraid." (Mk. 10.32).

If Mark had the women disciples come to anoint the body on the
"third day" so that he could contrast their foolishness with the understanding of the women at Bethany, we need to look for another reason
for the visit of the women to the tomb.

Burial customs in the New Testament period differed little from those
in the preceding centuries. Luke mentions the washing and laying out of
Tabitha (Acts 9.37) and he reports that, when Ananias died, a group of
"young men rose and wrapped him up and carried him out and buried
him" (Acts 5.6). The period of mourning normally lasted seven days

(Gen. 50.10, 1 Sam. 31.13, 1 Chron. 10.12, Sirach 22.12). This was a time of prayer and fasting but the third day was special. The first three days were known as "the days of weeping." Talking was forbidden. It was thought that death was not final until the third day. The last four days of mourning were called "the days of lamentation."[164] It was then that the decomposition of the body began. This time of mourning and fasting would be interrupted by a funeral feast, a gathering of friends and family. It might be held during a visit to the tomb on the third day. Jeremiah tells us of a day of doom when people will die without the proper rites being performed "they shall not be buried and no one shall lament for them or cut himself or make himself bald for them, no one shall break bread for the mourner, to comfort him for the dead, nor shall any one give him a cup of consolation to drink for his father or his mother" (Jer. 16.6, 7).

All four gospels record the discovery of the empty tomb by "women." It is difficult to imagine that the early Church would have invented such a narrative in a society in which a woman's testimony was of much less value than that of a man.

This report by the "the women" that the tomb was empty made it possible for the disciples, within a very short time, to preach the resurrection of Jesus. They made this claim in a society that believed that the resurrection involved the dead body. This is the point of Ezekiel's vision of the dry bones coming together (Ezek. 37.7–10) and the mention of bodies once "in the tombs" coming forth in resurrection (Matt. 27.52, 53, Jn. 5.28, 29). Even the Jewish response to the preaching of the resurrection at the time of Matthew did not deny the claim that the tomb was empty (Matt. 28.13–15).

Bultmann and others reject these arguments, indeed they reverse them. They claim that the story was developed so that the gospel could be preached to people who believed that resurrection involved the raising of bodies.[165] These stories then grew out of the preaching of the resurrection. Grass tells us that these stories are only part of a tendency that we see in the later gospels to emphasize the corporeality of the raised Jesus.[166] It is difficult to believe that the particular reports of the events at the tomb that we now have can be seen as stories that were developed to support the resurrection message.

It seems likely then that on that "third day" at the tomb, the women were about to break their fast. Two of the gospels tell us that Jesus appeared to the women at the tomb. There may be a third gospel report of such an event. Luke may refer to such an incident in 24.24. "They did not see" could refer to the women or "those with us." If it is taken as referring to the women it would mean that Luke explicitly denied that there was an appearance at the tomb. On the other hand, it is much more likely that "those with us" is the subject of the sentence and this would imply that although the women had seen Jesus the others did not share the experience. In Matthew 28.9, 10 we have a short report that tells of Mary Magdalene and the other Mary meeting Jesus. Jesus repeats the message of the angel except that the angel's message was for the disciples whereas this message is for "my brethren." Perhaps in this way Matthew is showing that he is aware of both the Jerusalem and Galilee traditions. The Johannine tradition also shows an awareness of the two traditions. In John's gospel Jesus appears to Mary Magdalene alone (Jn. 20.11–18), although John 20.2 implies that there were other women with her. She fails to recognize Jesus at first. Again there is a message from Jesus for "my brethren." She had originally run to tell Peter and the other disciples, not "the brethren" about the empty tomb.

All the New Testament tradition about the resurrection remembers that Jesus "was buried, that he was raised on the third day" (1 Cor. 15.4). All the gospel writers remember that "the women" were the first to report that "he was alive" (Lk. 24.23). The women remained in Jerusalem to complete the traditional seven days of mourning, led by Mary Magdalene. On the third day, the day they would break their fast, they came to the tomb early in the morning. The reports are confusing. Every report is different. In some reports men disciples appear. In some reports Jesus appears. Some reports can be described as angelophanies. Angels, in scripture express and interpret events in God's world. The people reading the gospels would know that they were a literary device that explained the special enlightenment that the women had received. The reaction of amazement and uncertainty is typical of angelophanies. The point of all the stories is that the disciples of Jesus are to be told that Jesus had risen from the dead and that he would soon appear to them. Whether the message came from Jesus or an angel we cannot tell. Perhaps the days of fasting when they had "mourned and wept" (Mk. 16.10) had had their effect, but on the "third day," the day of the funeral feast, the message came that "he was alive" (Lk. 24.23).

2. The Appearances in Galilee

The report of the women who visited the tomb on "the third day" was that Jesus was alive. Their task was to tell the disciples. The persistence of the Galilean appearance motif through all the gospels and its connection with the appearances to the twelve is surely significant. Apparently, Galilee was the destination of the women's message. Even Luke, who puts all the appearances in Jerusalem, probably for his own theological reasons, mentions Galilee and changes the reference to what has occurred in the past. The earliest tradition after 1 Corinthians 15 is that of Mark 16.7, which leads one to believe that an appearance to Peter and the twelve took place in Galilee. That seems to be where the disciples fled, as John 16.32 put it, "The hour is coming, indeed it has come, when you will be scattered every man to his home." The appearances recorded in Matthew 28.16–20 to the eleven and in John 21 to the seven are set in Galilee.

If there were no separate appearance to Peter, we can explain why Matthew drops the mention of Peter from his version of Mark 16.7. Matthew has the angels say to the women "go quickly and tell his disciples" (Matt. 28.7) rather than Mark's "tell his disciples and Peter." In Matthew, Peter is the usual spokesman for the disciples although he is never placed above the others. This suggestion also means that there is no need to argue that various stories such as Peter's call in Luke Chapter 5, or Peter's confession of the Messiahship of Jesus in Matthew 16, conceal what had once been accounts of Peter's private resurrection experience. There is no doubt that the resurrection influenced the telling of the gospel stories and some stories may preserve features that have been lost in the resurrection narrative. Mark makes a connection between the resurrection and the transfiguration in Mark 9.9, 10 in that certain features, the mountain and the glowing white garments, are like a resurrection scene. Yet it is only the prominence of Peter and the absence of any account of his private encounter with Jesus that make these suggestions attractive. The same can be said about the account in Luke 5.1–11 that tells of the miraculous draft of fishes and the calling of the disciples in Mark 1.16–20. It must be admitted, however, that Peter's reaction in Luke 5.8 "Depart from me for I am a sinful man" seems appropriate in a post-resurrection context. The only passage implying that there may have been a separate appearance to Peter is Luke 24.34. The two disciples return from Emmaus and before they can tell their story, the disciples tell them "The Lord has risen indeed and has appeared to Simon." Yet even here we are not told that Peter was apart from the group when Jesus appeared. The disciples seem to have shared in the event as they are so certain.

The use of the word "Cephas" for Peter in 1 Corinthians 15 is significant. We are told in Matthew 16.17–19 that the name Peter or *Petros*,
the "rock" was bestowed on Simon Bar-jona, the promised foundation
stone of the Church. That small group was also promised by Jesus that
"They would sit on twelve thrones judging the twelve tribes of Israel"
(Matt. 19.28). It seems that the appearance to Peter and the small group
of disciples in Galilee reestablished that group. The immediate result of
that appearance was the foundation of the Church of God.

In Paul's list in 1 Corinthians 15, there are three appearances linked
together in the first group before the interjection about those who have
died. These are the appearances to "Cephas, then to the twelve, then he
appeared to more than five hundred brethren." We have to note that in
John 21.7 it is Peter who first reacts to the presence of Jesus on shore.
So it is in the narratives of the visits to the empty tomb in Luke and
John. The way the passage in 1 Corinthians 15 is written, with Cephas
and the twelve sharing a single "he appeared" we may understand the
appearance to Peter to be nothing more than this, that he was the first of
the group to recognize Jesus. Only in John 21 does the Beloved Disciple
first see that it is Jesus, as he is the first to "believe" at the tomb, but
this seems to be the result of John's special theological interest in the relationship between Peter and the "Beloved Disciple." As Peter had in
the past acted as spokesman for the group and as leader of the inner
membership, so Peter was the first to "see" Jesus in the experience of
the resurrection meal. This may explain why there is no record of a separate appearance to Peter and why there is no suggestion that, after a
separate appearance, Peter organized the group so that he could explain
what happened.

We have noted the parallelism in Paul's list in 1 Corinthians 15. Apparently Paul received his information first hand when he went to Jerusalem to enquire of Cephas and James (Gal. 1.18, 19). He must also
have spoken to one or more of the "More than five hundred brethren"
to obtain his report on the events that followed the appearance to Cephas
and the twelve. He suggests that any doubter could check on this report
as most of them are "still alive, though some have fallen asleep."

Paul probably wrote his first letter to the Corinthians sometime in the
fifties AD. It was his intention in this passage to attack those who would
deny the resurrection. Paul did this by listing the historical record of
events that he had "received" soon after his conversion. This could be
just a year or two after the events themselves, in the early thirties AD.

Paul took parts of the formulas that he has "received" and put them in an orderly list with the resurrection appearances. It is unlikely that in 1 Corinthians 15.3b–5 we see the complete tradition of the events in Jerusalem that Paul was taught on his conversion. It seems more likely that individual parts of what had become a formula were connected together by Paul. The language is not Pauline; it has a "creedal" quality. The repetition of "and that" may well be the work of Paul. The appearances that are listed have been put in sequence and connected by "then" or "afterward." They may have been lists that supported the special authority of an individual or group in the early Church. Paul organized these traditions so that he is seen as one of those Christians honored by an appearance. Paul's purpose may best be seen when we set out the passage in a more literal translation.

v. 3   For I delivered to you as of *first importance*
          what I also received
          that Christ died for our sins...

v. 4   *and that* he was buried
          and that he was raised...

v. 5   *and that* he appeared to Cephas
          then to the twelve

v. 6   *Afterward*... to more than 500 brethren
          once for all

v. 7   *afterward* he appeared to James
          then to all the apostles

v. 8   *Last of all*... he appeared
          also to me

We have emphasized the word "that." It is repeated four times before the statements about death, burial, resurrection and the appearances. Paul seems to use *hoti* or "that" to combine different traditions in the same way we would use quotation marks. The word is used in much the same manner in 1 Thessalonians 4.13–17. As we have noted, Paul probably combined parts of what he had received in this way.

All the other words we have emphasized are words showing that Paul intended to set these events in chronological order (first, then, afterward, once for all, afterward, then, last of all). We have translated the word normally translated as "at one time" in the same way that it is translated when it is used in other places in the New Testament. It is used in Romans 6.10 to mean "once for all." The only other place the word is used in the New Testament, in Hebrews 7.27, 9.12, and 10.10, it is used in this way. Paul has two other words that he uses when he means "at one time" as in 2 Corinthians 11.25 ("Once was I stoned") or Romans 7.9 ("I was alive without the law once"). Our word is translated "at one time" only because it is seen as referring to the five hundred as a part of a series. Yet if we see the word as ending the first section of a report we should translate the word "once for all." It then becomes part of a series of words that set all the events in chronological order. We will see the importance of this translation when we come to study the place of the "more than five hundred brethren" in our resurrection reports.

Matthew begins his resurrection chapter with an account of a visit "to see the sepulchre" by Mary Magdalene and the other Mary. They encounter an angel who tells them to tell the disciples that Jesus is "going before them to Galilee" (Matt. 28.7). As they are on their way to the disciples they are met by Jesus and he tells them to tell the brethren to go to Galilee. Matthew seems certain that the main resurrection appearance took place in Galilee.

When we come to the report of the appearance to the eleven, we find a very terse summary report of the event. We are not told about the setting or the reaction of the disciples, except the phrase "but some doubted" (Matt. 28.17). We are told that the disciples went to "the mountain to which Jesus had directed them" (Matt. 28.16). Since there has been no mention of this mountain in the messages given to the women we must assume that it is a mountain that has special significance to the disciples.

"The mountain" is a special place for Matthew. He removes casual references to mountains that he finds in Mark. For instance, in the story of the Gerasene demoniac he removes the reference that Mark makes to the mountains (Mk. 5.5, 11). He also removes the scene in which Jesus calls his disciples on the mountain so that he can place his emphasis on their training on the mountain (Matt. 5.1, 2). But Matthew also adds references to "the mountain." Only in Matthew is it the place where the shepherd goes to look for his lost sheep (Matt. 18.12). Only in Matthew is the saying about faith that can move mountains repeated twice (Matt. 17.20, 21.21). Matthew keeps the connection between the feeding of the five thousand and the mountain (Matt. 14.23) but when he comes to tell of the feeding of the four thousand, the setting is described in the same language as the setting of the Sermon on the Mount, "and he went up into the mountain and sat down" (Matt. 15.29, not "hills" as the R.S.V.). Only in Matthew do the "lame, the maimed, the blind, the dumb" come to the mountain to be healed (Matt. 15.29f). Only in Matthew does Jesus view the "kingdoms of the world" from a "very high mountain" (Matt. 4.8). The transfiguration and the events on the Mount of Olives completes Matthew's references to the mountain.

When Matthew gives us his summary of the resurrection appearance to the disciples at "the mountain to which Jesus directed them" (Matt. 28.16), those who had read his gospel would know that this appearance was taking place where Jesus, in the past, had taught the law of the New Commandment and where he had "blessed and broke and gave the loaves to the disciples and the disciples gave them to the crowds" (Matt. 14.19 and very nearly 15.36).

This final scene in Matthew's gospel should not be seen apart from the broader context. The gospel opens with events that recall the birth and childhood of Moses.[167] The baptism of Jesus by John parallels Israel's passing through the waters. Then follows the temptations in the wilderness which occur in the same order in Matthew as they do in the Old Testament. Then in Chapter 5.1 and 2, Jesus, like Moses, sits on the mountain, the mount of revelation, the mount of the new law.[168] Again we have the connection between the law and eating, the connection between Elim and Sinai (Ex. 16), the Sermon on the Mount and the Feeding of the Five Thousand. We must also remember that the story of Moses and Matthew's story of Jesus both end on mountains. From his final mountain of Nebo, Moses is able to look at all the land that is an inheritance of the twelve tribes of Israel (Deut. 34). In Matthew the eleven disciples are made to look toward "all nations" (Matt. 28.19). In a Jewish work written about the time of Jesus we have a similar theme. In the Assumption of Moses, the twelve tribes are promised that "thou shalt look down from on high and shall see thy enemies in Gehenna" (Ass. of M. 10.10).

Perhaps only Matthew knew of a final commissioning of the disciples by Jesus in Galilee. He supplied the setting for the scene, a scene that would remind his readers that the disciples' mission was to teach the word and the sacraments in "the name of the Father and of the Son and of the Holy Spirit" (Matt. 28.19). If Matthew's setting of the appearance of Jesus was formed by his theology, perhaps the other report that we have of an appearance in Galilee gives us a better picture of the actual event.

The final verses of John Chapter 20 read as though they were meant to be the conclusion of the gospel. Now we have another final chapter that tells of an appearance in Galilee. The style of Chapter 21 is very like the rest of the gospel and it deals with themes already mentioned in the gospel, especially the relationship between Peter and the Beloved Disciple. The chapter shows Peter and the Beloved Disciple as partners and it shows that the writer of the chapter felt that the Galilean supper tradition should not be ignored in any account of the resurrection.

It is rather strange to find the disciples who have been sent in mission, in the power of the Holy Spirit (Jn. 20.21, 22) spending their time fishing in Galilee. Stranger still, if these seven have gone through the doubting Thomas episode, that they do not recognize Jesus as he stands on the beach. We again have all the elements of other resurrection stories. It takes place in the morning, there is a lack of recognition, then there is a sudden insight that it is the Lord, and it all takes place in the context of a meal. In this account there are many similarities with the story of the miraculous draft of fishes found in Luke 5. It is the disciple that Jesus loved who first recognizes Jesus, but again it is Peter who is first to act. When the disciples come to land they find that a breakfast of fish and bread has already been prepared and they are called to share in the meal. The words in John 21.13 'Jesus came and took the bread and gave it to them and so with the fish" are very like the words in John 6.11 at the feeding of the five thousand. *Codex Bezae* heightens the similarity by adding the word for giving thanks, *eucharistesas*. These words, the setting and the meal, the only two meals aside from the wedding feast at Cana mentioned in John's gospel, mean that his teaching on the "bread of life" in Chapter 6 applies to both passages.

The resurrection meal in Galilee has been used in the Johanine parabolic manner. The disciples follow their Lord's direction and cast their net on the "right" side and find they are unable to haul it in. The word used for haul is the same word that is used in John 6.44 "No one can come to me unless the Father who sent me *draws* him." When they come to land they find that Jesus can feed them without their aid, yet he asks for some of their fish. When they draw the net to shore, it does not break even though it is filled with 153 large fish, of which not one needs to be thrown back. The passage tells us that the disciples task as fishers of men will be miraculously successful if they obey the Lord's commands, remain in his fellowship, recognize his presence and receive sustenance from him.

The writer of John Chapter 21 seems to have combined two stories. One tells of the recognition of Jesus by the disciples in a meal on the Galilean shore. The other tells of a miraculous draft of fishes and this story is very like the story in Luke Chapter 5. If we remove the verses that belong to the "meal" theme, we have a simple resurrection scene: "After this Jesus revealed himself again to the disciples by the sea of Tiberias. Just as day was breaking, Jesus stood on the beach; yet the disciples did not know it was Jesus. When they got out on land they saw a charcoal fire there, with fish lying on it and bread. Jesus said to them 'Come and have breakfast.' Now none of the disciples dared ask him 'Who are you?' They knew it was the Lord. Jesus came and took the bread and gave it to them, and so with the fish."

If this report in John 21 and the resurrection scene at the end of Matthew's gospel tell us of the appearance to "Cephas, then to the twelve," what about the appearance to the "more than five hundred brethren?" Our suggestion is that they are those who came to share in the mission endeavor in Galilee. The small group re-formed by the appearance of Jesus began to tell others the good news of the gospel.

These "special" resurrection appearances of Jesus had to come to an end sometime. Mark avoids the question of when by not giving any account of the resurrection. Matthew ends his gospel with an appearance on the mountain and the promise "Lo, I am with you always, to the close of the age" (Matt. 28.20). Luke's appearances end in forty days with the Ascension. John speaks of the Ascension of Jesus but he ends with the promise of Jesus to "come" (John 21.23) and a blessing on those "who have not seen and yet believe" (John 20.29). By telling us that the appearances to the "more than five hundred" were "once and for all," Paul was saying that those "special" appearances in Galilee had come to an end.

The picture we are given by Paul in this list of what we suggest are the Galilean appearances to Peter, to the small group and then to a larger group of disciples, is most likely a picture of the leadership of the Galilean Church at the time that Paul wrote the epistle. As Karl Barth states, Paul, in this passage, was telling the Corinthians that the gospel he had preached to them was the same gospel that had been preached by the other leaders of the Church.[169] Paul is therefore making a claim to the same authority, claiming recognition of his own leadership. He tells us that he has had the same experience and has preached the same gospel as all the other leaders of the Church.

Paul speaks of his own experience as being "the last of all" the appearances. What must be meant is that this appearance to "one untimely born" ended the special appearances that had revealed the eschatological and Christological significance of Jesus. This group of more than five hundred would have been seen by Peter and the disciples as the confirmation of their experience. As they broke bread together with some of the people to whom Jesus had preached in Galilee, Jesus appeared in their midst. These events were seen as the founding of the Christian Church. There is no need to picture a gathering of "more than five hundred" at which Jesus appeared. There could well have been a series of events as the disciples shared with others what had happened.

What took place in Galilee? We know from 1 Corinthians 15 that the first appearances of Jesus were to Peter and the twelve. It is likely that these appearances took place in Galilee. Perhaps some of the reports that we have of appearances to the disciples in Jerusalem or nearby originated from reports of the events in Galilee. The setting could have been changed for theological reasons. We now have only two accounts of the appearances in Galilee. Matthew's account, set for his own theological reasons on the mount of revelation, near or at the place of the miraculous feeding, is not really so much an appearance account as it is a Matthean theological statement. Fuller points to the large number of Mattheanisms and suggests that he has combined three separate logia.[170] Matthew may well have had to write an account of what he understood had happened in Galilee. The appearance of Jesus was a commission to mission. He ends his account with the promise "Lo, I am with you always, to the close of the age" (Matt. 28.20). This verse parallels another saying of Jesus recorded in Matt. 18.20, "For where two or three are gathered in my name there am I in the midst of them." The promise of Emmanuel, God with us (Matt. 1.23) is given to the infant Church when it gathers to worship, when it gathers to "break bread." Jesus promised his presence, as he was present that day with his small group in Galilee.

The other report that we have of the events in Galilee is set by a lakeside. Without the story of the miraculous draft of fishes we have a straightforward account of a meal. Jesus invites the disciples to "Come and have breakfast." Then we are told that the disciples dare not ask "who are you?" The meaning of this question becomes clear when we run the next two verses together. "They knew it was the Lord, Jesus came and took the bread and gave it to them, and so with the fish" (Jn.

21.12b, 13). Jesus here is not demonstrating that he is the host. He performs the eucharistic actions of taking and giving the bread. All this is set in Galilee by the writer of this chapter so that we may see the beginnings of the mission of the Church under the leadership of Peter. Fuller sums up his detailed study of this chapter in these words, "The Johannine traditions add little to our historical knowledge of the Easter events though, at some places, especially in Chapter 21, they are in surprisingly close contact with the earliest tradition. Here they confirm the Galilean location, the eucharistic setting, and the church-founding significance of the primary appearances to Peter and the twelve."[171] In the list of appearances in 1 Corinthians, Paul finishes his account of the happenings in Galilee "once for all" and proceeds to tell of events placed in and about Jerusalem.

3. The Appearances in Jerusalem

Luke's determination to write an "orderly account" (Lk. 1.3) of the "things which have been accomplished among us" (Lk. 1.1) has led him to concentrate all the Easter events in Jerusalem. One can find in Luke-Acts a parallel between the telling of the Christian story and geographical movement. There is a ministry of wondrous deeds associated with Galilee and a journey "up to Jerusalem and everything that is written of the Son of Man by the prophets will be accomplished" (Lk. 18.31). From there, the message of Jesus travels to all the world and to Rome where Paul spends his time "preaching the kingdom of God and teaching about the Lord Jesus Christ quite openly and unhindered" (Acts 28.31).

To begin with, Luke changes the angelic tidings to the women from Mark's promise of a Galilean future to the remembrance of a Galilean past. To emphasize the point, the women named are those mentioned when he told the story of their support of the twelve in Galilee (Lk. 8.1–3). The women, "returning from the tomb told all this to the eleven and to all the rest" (Lk. 24.9). The language is very Lukan, the word for return is used here and in twenty other places in Luke but it is never used in other gospels. The image of the eleven as a leadership group residing in Jerusalem surrounded by a larger group representing the Church shows the eleven at the center of the Easter events. Some disciples set out from this leadership group (Lk. 24.12f) but they soon return. It is Luke who is concerned to record the restoration of the group to twelve in Acts 1.21–26. They are the collegial "witnesses of the resurrection." Peter is still given a leadership role, he runs to the tomb (accepting verse twelve as authentic), but he returns baffled. Later (Lk. 24.34) we learn that Jesus has appeared to Peter but we are not given an account of the meeting.

The Emmaus story is the longest and most detailed of all the resurrection stories. There is a lengthy dialogue between the stranger and the two disciples as they walk along the way. They reflect on the scripture and the passion and death of Jesus. The whole passage builds to the supper scene. The stranger takes the role of the host and the reenactment of the meals they have shared with their earthly master ends their blindness, "their eyes were opened and they recognized him" (Lk. 24.31). All through his writing, Luke connects instruction about the person and mission of Jesus with the meals he had with his disciples (Lk. 9.16, 22.19). That pattern continues in this scene and in others in Acts (1.3f, 2.46). In this personal encounter, Jesus lifts the veil and the disciples "see." The passive form of the verbs show that it is the risen Christ who reveals the meaning of his earthly "journey." That revelation does not come to the disciples because they now understand the scripture. It comes because Jesus chooses to reveal himself, after he has explained the mystery of his person. The means that he uses to open the eyes of faith is the breaking of bread. The suggestion, in what may be a summary of the Emmaus story that we find in Mark 16.12, that he appeared in "another form" is probably the result of a later writer missing the point of the "hiddenness" of Jesus.

Luke continues the story, again emphasizing time and place, (Lk. 24.33) when the two disciples return to "the eleven gathered together and those who were with them" at their evening meal. Before the travellers can speak they are told in the creedal language of the early Church "The Lord has risen indeed and has appeared to Simon" Jesus has revealed himself to the one who could only look into the tomb and "wonder" what had happened (Lk. 24.12). While the disciples are telling their tale they come to realize that Jesus stood among them. Again the disciples are startled and frightened. They have not yet realized that he is always to be with them and that he is not subject to space and time. Again Luke combines a meal with his disciples and instruction about his person and mission. This time, however, the food is taken from the disciples. Luke seems to picture Jesus as a missionary moving from community to community and accepting the food provided, as Jesus had instructed the seventy to do (Lk. 10.7). When he comes to write about the first mission to the gentiles in Acts 10, Luke pictures Peter in just such a situation. It is natural then that Peter would recall the example of his risen Lord. After a rehearsal of the facts about the mission and person of Jesus, we are told that "God raised him on the third day and made him manifest; not to all the people but to us who were chosen by God as witnesses, who ate and drank with him after he rose from the dead" (Acts 10.40, 41). Again we have a similar combination in the introduction to Acts. Jesus is described as having "presented himself alive" to the chosen apostles, "speaking of the kingdom of God and eating with them" (Acts 1.3b, 4a). The word that is usually translated "staying," *sunalizomenos*, as in the R.S.V. means literally "taking salt with." Modern Greeks have a saying "We have eaten bread and salt together," which they take to mean that we have shared the most elemental foods, suffered hardships and yet known the same joys so much so that not even death can break these bonds. The "persuasive proofs" spoken about in Acts 1.3 seems to be this combination of word and action. Luke ends his gospel with the commissioning of the "witnesses" including the eleven and "those who were with them" (Lk. 24.33).

The Jerusalem tradition that is preserved in John 20.19–25 and 26–29 is again a meal tradition. The indication of evening as the time of the meal is traditional. Indeed the action has been separated into two meals, one on the evening of "the first day of the week" and then, to complete the Thomas story, another occasion a week later.[172] There are many similarities between these passages and the Lukan tradition. In both we have a meal appearance preceded by a reference to another appearance. In Luke 24.34, the eleven and those that were with them report "The Lord has risen indeed and has appeared to Simon." In John 20.18 we have Mary Madgalene's report to the brethren "I have seen the Lord." In both Jesus encounters his earthly associates and greets them with the conventional Jewish greeting "Peace be with you," if we can accept Luke 24.36b. This ordinary greeting came to have a permanent place in the Christian eucharistic liturgy. Next, according to both gospels, Jesus deals with the disciples' uncertainty about the identity of the person before them. He then commissions them to mission, for the forgiveness of sins, in the power of the Holy Spirit (Lk. 24.47, Jn. 20.22f).

One of the similarities between these passages in Luke and John needs further attention. The words these gospel writers use to identify the risen one are very alike. In Luke 24 we have "Lord Jesus" (verse 3), in most ancient texts, "Jesus" (verse 15), and "Lord" (verse 34).

In John 20 we have "Jesus" (verses 19, 21, 24, 26, 29) and "Lord" (verses 20, 25, 28). We can see that the use of the proper name "Jesus" is to emphasize the identity and continuity between what is now taking place and the ministry of the earthly Jesus. However, aside from John's use of "Rabbi" (verse 16) and "My Lord and my God" (verse 28), the use of the word "Lord" in these scenes may have a eucharistic connection and therefore a connection with eating together. The formal "Lord Jesus" as we find it in 1 Corinthians 11.23 seems to be the central confession of the Hellenistic Church as "Jesus is Lord" was possibly the earliest baptismal creed (Rom. 10.9, Phil. 2.11). The use of the word "Lord" already had a place in the Palestinian, Aramaic environment of the early Church. During Jesus' lifetime we are told that the disciples called Jesus "Master and Lord" (Jn. 13.13). The transmission of the Aramaic eucharistic formula *Maranatha* without translation shows the importance of this expression. The most natural place for it to have come into use would have been at the "meals" of the risen One. It is used in connection with the eucharist in 1 Corinthians 16.22, Revelation 22.20 and at the close of a prayer in the Didache. In those resurrection meals the disciples were reunited with the Lord they had come to know and love in the past. *Maranatha,* Our Lord comes. In those meals the disciples experienced the joy of the victory over death. *Maranatha,* Our Lord had come. In those meals the disciples longed for the complete coming at the end of time. *Maranatha,* Our Lord, Come. The difficulty over how this phase should be translated is solved if we see it used in this setting. The use of "Lord Jesus" in the resurrection scenes in Luke and John stems from the disciples' meals with the risen Jesus.

Just who was present at these meals? Jesus told Mary Magdalene to "go to my brethren and say to them" (Jn. 20.17), much as he told the women in Matthew "Go and tell my brethren" (Matt. 28.10). From then on the reference is to "the disciples." Because Simon Peter and "the other disciple" have run to the tomb we can assume that they are present. It is sometimes assumed that, because Thomas is described as "one of the twelve" (Jn. 20.24), it is only the eleven who are present at these meals. The phrase may mean exactly the opposite. In John's gospel there is no sense of a ruling group at "Church Headquarters" in Jerusalem. The phrase "one of the twelve" then should be seen as saying that among a much larger group there was "one of the twelve." This larger group in Jerusalem would have consisted, first of all, of the women who had followed Jesus from Galilee. Prominent among these women was Mary, the mother of Jesus. Living with Mary and travelling with her were the brothers and sisters of Jesus (Jn. 2.12, 7.3, Matt. 12.46, 13.55). Whether they were actual brothers and sisters or were some other relations, they were family. Like many families, they seemed to have been jealous of Jesus and refused to accept his claims. The gospels represent Jesus as lamenting the unbelief and want of sympathy of his own family, "A prophet is not without honor, except in his own country and among his own kin and in his own house" (Mk. 6.4). John tells us that "even his brothers did not believe in him" (Jn. 7.5). Mark 3.21 tells us that "when his friends heard it, they went out to seize him for they said he is beside himself." The word translated "friends" in the R.S.V. should more probably be translated "family," as in the N.E.B. None of this group was numbered among the twelve. They are always distinguished from the twelve as they are in Acts 1.14 where the twelve "together with the women and Mary the mother of Jesus and with his brothers" are regarded as separate groups who yet are in one accord.

It was the resurrection that changed this relationship. The record that we have in John 20 of an appearance to the disciples in Jerusalem is a record of an appearance to the "brethren" and the family of Jesus. Luke also records an appearance in Jerusalem but he limits it to the eleven and the two disciples from the supper at Emmaus. Apparently, it was James the Lord's brother (Gal. 1.19) who came to be the leader of this Jerusalem group. As we have seen with the appearance to Peter and the twelve, Paul may have meant in 1 Corinthians 15.5 that this took place in a single disclosure. He may also have meant that there was only a single appearance to James and others. There is no need to suggest that we do not have accounts of a separate appearance to Peter or James if we agree that they were simply the first to react to the presence of Jesus at an appearance to a number of disciples.

James is called an apostle by Paul (Gal. 1.19). On one occasion he is listed before Peter as one of the chief pillars of the Church (Gal. 2.9). It is James that presides and announces the decision at the Council of Jerusalem even though Peter is present (Acts 15.13). His importance is shown in the delegates he sent to Antioch (Gal. 2.12) and passages such as Acts 12.17 and 21.18. James is called an apostle in the wider sense in which the term is applied to Paul himself, to Barnabas (Acts 14.4–14, 1 Cor. 9.6), to Andronicus and Junias (Rom. 16.7). It is these apostles, distinguished from the small group formed by Jesus, that Paul puts in his list in 1 Corinthians 15.7. He then lists himself as the culmination of

this group. He listed himself as one of this company of apostles, the last
and the least of the apostles.

James then, was the first of "all the apostles" to "see" the Lord.
Paul had a much longer list of apostles than the small group formed by
Jesus. We read of missionaries to Phoenicia, Cyprus and Antioch (Acts
11.19) and of the seven we are told about in Acts Chapter 6 who may
have been part of this larger group. If there were, as is likely, groups of
Aramaic-speaking Jewish Christians and groups of Hellenistic Jewish
Christians, both groups at times called apostles, we can understand why
Paul speaks of "all the apostles."

We have noticed that the reports of the appearances in Jerusalem in
Luke-Acts and John picture others present at the meals with Jesus beside the small group originally formed by Jesus. Just as Thomas "one of
the twelve" appeared at the supper a week after the other gathering of
disciples, so after the experience in Galilee, other members of the
twelve apparently returned to Jerusalem. It was here that the early
Christian mission began. It was here that these early missionary
Apostles, chosen by God as witnesses, "ate and drank with him after he
rose from the dead" (Acts 10.41).

The last of our "Jerusalem" appearances was the appearance to Paul.
Luke tells us that although Paul was born in Tarsus he was brought up
and educated in Jerusalem (Acts 22.3, 26.4). His family lived there
(Acts 23.16). In the three versions we are given of Paul's conversion
experience we are told that it happened as he left Jerusalem and
"journeyed to Damascus with the authority and commission of the chief
priests" (Acts 26.12). The other versions, Acts 9.1f and 22.6f, are similar. There are inconsistencies within these three versions. In one,
Paul's companions "stood speechless, hearing the voice but seeing no
one" (Acts 9.6). In another, they "saw the light but did not hear the
voice" (Acts 22.9), whereas in a third, they all fall to the ground when
they see the light but only Paul hears the voice (Acts 26.14). The much
more important inconsistencies are between these reports and what Paul
himself tells us of his experience. The one point that Paul consistently
makes is that he saw the Lord (Gal. 1.11–16, 1 Cor. 9.1, 2, 15.3–11).
Yet, these accounts in Acts virtually exclude that possibility. The
account that does tell of the appearance of Jesus to Paul is set in
Jerusalem: "When I had returned to Jerusalem and was praying in the
temple, I fell in a trance and saw him saying to me, "Make haste and
get quickly out of Jerusalem, because they will not accept your testi-

mony about me' " (Acts 22.17, 18). This passage assumes that Paul had no previous call to carry the message of Christ to the gentiles. It may be that the experience of the Damascus road was what Paul would call "visions and revelations of the Lord" (2 Cor. 12.1) or "the abundance of revelations" (2 Cor. 12.7) or a "revelation" (Gal. 1.12). He always makes a distinction between these experiences and the experience of seeing the Lord. He is very certain that the Lord appeared to him just as he had appeared to the other apostles and disciples. He seems to have seen this experience as a private matter for he tells us very little about it, yet he is certain that it was not a vision or a revelation. It was an actual appearance of the Lord. Although his experience came later it was similar to the experience of Peter and the others on his list. It made him a witness of the resurrection and therefore made him qualified to be "an apostle not from men nor through men but through Jesus Christ and God the Father, who raised him from the dead" (Gal. 1.1).

The only report we have then of Paul seeing the Lord is the passage telling of his experience in the temple at Jerusalem. It is difficult to reconcile this account with what we are told in Acts 9.26–30 about Paul's return to Jerusalem, when Barnabas introduced him to the apostles and he explained how "on the road he had seen the Lord, who spoke to him" (Acts 9.27). It is also difficult to reconcile these accounts with what Paul tells us in Galatians. The point Paul is making in this letter is that his call was independent of those in Jerusalem. He does not actually tell us that his conversion took place at Damascus, we only assume that because he speaks of a return to Damascus (Gal. 1.17). He may mean that he returned to where he first preached the gospel.

We can only speculate about when or where Paul experienced an appearance of Jesus. Luke may be correct in separating Paul's conversion experience from the time he "saw him." Some have suggested that Luke was trying to heal a breach that already existed in the Church of that early period.[173] Yet, Galatians and Acts agree, however, that the experience that Paul had of seeing the Lord led him to begin his great mission to preach Christ among the gentiles (Gal. 1.16, Acts 22.21).

Luke ends the "special" appearances of Jesus to the eleven "together with the women and Mary the mother of Jesus and his brothers" (Acts 1.14) after forty days. He does not tell us of appearances to James or to Paul and the apostles. John Knox has shown that the chronology derived from Paul's own writing is to be preferred to the rather different chronology derived from Acts.[174] Perhaps the same could be said of the chronology of the appearances. Paul's list, more personal and more primitive, is to be preferred.

We do not have a record of the appearance "to James, then to all the apostles." We must assume that they were part of the Jerusalem appearances. That experience changed their lives. It was a conversion experience. Very soon James and others were involved with Paul in the mission of the Church (Gal. 1.19, 2.1–12, Acts 15.13f, 21.18).

What then was the nature of these appearances in Jerusalem as they are reported by Luke and John? The one theme found consistently through all the reports is that of the presence of Jesus at a meal with his disciples.

Much has been written about the background of the longest and most detailed of the appearance stories, the walk to Emmaus. Fuller lists the various suggestions that have been made about the literary and artistic background of this composition of Luke. He makes the point that "Behind this portrait there is also authentic Christian experience: the Risen One made himself known to the disciples in the breaking of bread. In this motif there is enshrined a generation or more of Christian eucharistic worship (cf., the primitive liturgical acclamation, *Maranatha*) and behind it further the earliest understanding of the resurrection appearances as revelatory encounters."[175] Perhaps we have in this story a report of an appearance by Jesus to some of the group that Paul calls "all of the apostles." The name Cleopas does not appear among lists of early apostles, but it may have been a name known to those for whom Luke wrote his gospel.

It has been suggested that the appearance at Emmaus is in the context of an eucharistic meal and that this context is probably that of all or most of the resurrection appearances.[176] In this way the beginnings of Christian worship can be traced to those meals with the risen Lord. Eucharistic worship may have developed in this way, but the meal motif serves many purposes. We need to realize that the most important, primary purpose of those meals was the restoration of table-fellowship by Jesus with his disciples. After the crucifixion, Jesus made himself known by again eating with his followers. This is why almost every appearance report, aside from Matthew's summary, is set in the context of a meal. The longest and most detailed is the report of the walk to Emmaus but when the two disciples return to Jerusalem they find the disciples gathered at their evening meal. Again Jesus comes to "stand among them." We have noted the other references Luke has made in Acts (1.4, 10.41) to the presence of Jesus at meals. The addition to

Mark's gospel tells of the appearance to the eleven as they "sat at table" (Mk. 16.14). There are many such texts that would support the suggestion that Jesus restored his relationship with his disciples by sharing together with them in the "breaking of bread."

4. Conclusion

What we know about the ministry of Jesus has been shaped by the writers of the gospels. They wrote to instruct the Church of their time. They adapted the tradition that had been handed down to them to present a Jesus who was popular and successful. They picture him as being welcomed throughout Galilee by overwhelming crowds. Greeted by almost all the people of Jerusalem when he entered the city. So great was the number of people who came to be healed by Jesus he was forced to tell them that they were to "tell no one" (Lk. 5.14) and yet "great multitudes gathered to hear and to be healed of their infirmities." Indeed at the sermon on the "level place" a "great crowd of his disciples and a great multitude of people from all Judea and Jerusalem and the seacoast of Tyre and Sidon came to hear him and to be healed of their diseases" (Lk. 6.17). The evangelists present us with a popular preacher who taught the people in a straightforward manner in simple parables. The reaction of the people was that they glorified God saying "A great prophet has arisen among us" (Lk. 7.16). There were only a few who did not accept Jesus, "The chief priests and the scribes and the principal men of the people sought to destroy him but they did not find anything they could do, for all the people hung on his words" (Lk. 19.47, 48).

We have tried to suggest that much of this view is mistaken. We have argued that the way to understand the resurrection is to understand that much of the ministry of Jesus was directed at the "training of the twelve." We have suggested that during his ministry Jesus built with his disciples a meaning system or understanding of life. He formed with them what sociologists call a "small group." We found that the twelve met all the criteria for such a group. This group gradually came to realize that many of the elements of the promised future kingdom were present in their life with Jesus. They were being trained to live in and for that future.

This coming reign of God that Jesus proclaimed was something that was entirely God's own doing. It was not something that Jesus planned to bring to pass. It was a new age, a new beginning that would be brought by God. This coming of God's reign demanded a response, a response to God's unconditional mercy, grace and love. In a sense the eschatological judgement was already made (e.g., Mk. 8.38, 9.41). Then again that judgement will be made by the twelve for "as my Father appointed a kingdom for me so do I appoint a kingdom for you that you may eat and drink at my table in my kingdom, and sit on thrones judging the twelve tribes of Israel" (Lk. 22.29, 30). Jesus, speaking the definitive word of God, with authority (e.g., Mk. 1.22, 27), prepared the small group he had chosen for their task in the new age that was to come.

This small group was asked to "bear their cross," to be willing to accept martyrdom with Jesus. They were trained to participate in a healing ministry that they came to see as part of the proclamation of the coming age. They learned to pray always, to live constantly in God's presence. The parables were directed at the disciples, to encourage, warn and support that small group, to teach them about God, his kingdom and the new age to come. The Sermon on the Mount can be seen as a summary of the ethical teaching received by the group, as a rule of life. This was part of their training, as was eating with publicans and sinners, for the time when they would "sit on twelve thrones judging the twelve tribes of Israel" (Matt. 19.28). Finally we saw how Jesus made each evening meal with his disciples a special time apart when he reminded them what they faced by the way he "took bread, and blessed and broke it" (Mk. 14.22, par.).

This way of life was shattered by the crucifixion. The group that Jesus had formed to be with him disintegrated. Instead of facing martyrdom they denied that they even knew Jesus. As Jesus had foretold they scattered like sheep (Mk. 14.27). They had promised that they would be able to drink the bitter cup that Jesus would drink but when the time came they refused (Mk. 10.39). Mark tells us that they "forsook him and fled" (Mk. 14.50). Matthew adds that all the "disciples" forsook him and fled (Matt. 26.56). Their despair and denial is emphasized by the tale of the young man so determined to escape that he fled naked (Mk. 14.51), and by the detailed account of Peter's denial "I do not know this man" (Mk. 14.71).

Sociological study has shown that when the leader is removed or even when the leader is absent, a "small group" tends to fall apart. It often breaks into smaller groups.[177] In John's gospel we find Peter and six other disciples back in Galilee working as fishermen. Some of the twelve seem to have remained for a time in Jerusalem with other of the

former followers of Jesus. Instead of continuing a ministry of healing
and exorcism their confidence and authority seems to have deserted
them. Instead of continuing to live in God's presence, of retreating to a
life of prayer in some desert place, they returned to fishing. Instead of
living as forgiven men the ethics of the new age, they followed the
ethics of the business world of Galilee.

The twelve disciples had been like Simeon "righteous and devout,
looking for the consolation of Israel" (Lk. 2.25). The good news that
had attracted them to Jesus was his message that "the kingdom of God
was at hand" (Mk. 1.15). They had looked to share in that end-time
when they would "sit on twelve thrones judging the twelve tribes of Israel" (Matt. 19.28). Resurrection entered this picture but it was a resurrection that was part of the events that would come at the end of time. It
was never thought of as an event that would occur within history. It was
one of the many eschatological events. At the time of Jesus, belief in the
resurrection of the dead was shared by most Jews except the more conservative Sadducees. This belief in resurrection came as part of the
growth of an apocalyptic point of view. The Jews came to believe that
God would one day vindicate and reward the faithful ones who suffered
and died in persecution, particularly during the Maccabean struggle.
When the end came they looked for an end that would be outside of history when the righteous would rise from the dead to their reward and the
wicked would be raised to face their punishment.

The risen Jesus appears to his disciples within history. In the New
Testament the very same language used to tell of his miraculous healings, and even used to tell of the raising of Lazarus, is used to tell of the
resurrection of Jesus. There is no suggestion that his resurrection took
place outside the continuum of history. This is emphasized by the importance given to the phrase "on the third day." The reason we are told
again and again in the reports of the resurrection appearances that
"some doubted" (Matt. 28.17) is that what happened was completely
outside their comprehension. Here was an eschatological reality occur-
ring within the space-time continuum of their own lives. Again, the appearance stories constantly make the point that there is a real
correspondence between the person of Christ who is risen from the dead
and the Jesus the disciples had come to know and love before his death:
"then were the disciples glad when they saw the Lord" (Jn. 20.20).

Another element that we find in the appearance stories is that the disciples finally begin to understand the events that have taken place in
their life with Jesus. Things begin to fall in place, begin to have a depth

of meaning and a consistency that they never had before. This process continued through the writing of the gospels, and continues with the disciples of Jesus today. The twelve came to understand as Matthew puts it "that all authority in heaven and earth" had been given to Jesus (Matt. 28.18). Jesus explained to the two disciples as they walked to Emmaus the "necessity" of the events that led to the crucifixion (Lk. 24.25–27). Then with all the disciples "he opened their minds to understand the scriptures" (Lk. 24.45).

The disciples began to understand when part of the meaning system, part of the way of life that they had shared with Jesus was restored after "the third day." The part of the meaning system that was restored or reestablished by Jesus in the resurrection appearances was his familiar sharing with them in a common meal. The restoration of that meaning system began with the visit of "the women" to the tomb. The first part of the prescribed seven days of mourning, fasting and weeping were over. Perhaps the confusion in the reports of what actually happened at the tomb reflects the nervous excitement of that day. Every report is different. Mary Magdalene is the one consistent figure in all the events at the tomb. This "third day" may have been the day when those who had been fasting gathered, as Jeremiah put it "to break bread" and to "drink the cup of consolation" (Jer. 16.6, 7). The one consistent theme through all these reports is that "the women" must tell the others that Jesus is alive and that they must gather and await his appearance. "The women" were therefore the first witnesses to the resurrection.

The first part of the summary of the resurrection appearances that Paul sent to the Corinthians tells us that "he appeared to Cephas, then to the twelve, then he appeared to more than five hundred brethren" (1 Cor. 15.5, 6). The women at the tomb are told by the young man in white to "go tell his disciples and Peter that he is going before you to Galilee" (Mk. 16.7). Matthew has much the same message from the "angels of the Lord" except he removes the reference to Peter (Matt. 28.7). Luke changes the passage so that it becomes a remembrance of what had taken place in Galilee to bring the message in line with his own theology. In a chapter that has probably been added to John's gospel we are again told that "after this Jesus revealed himself again to the disciples by the sea of Tiberias" (Jn. 21.1). The support for a Galilean appearance tradition is so strong that we can only assume that Paul, in his report of the appearances to Peter, the twelve and the "more than five hundred" has given us the summary of that tradition.

Matthew's account tells us little about what took place. At "the mountain," so central in Matthew's gospel to the teaching of Jesus, a place connected with both the feedings of the multitude, the disciples of Jesus see him in the context of worship. We are not told that the appearance took place at a meal but we are told that some of the disciples did not "see" Jesus, that some of them "doubted." This is very like what takes place in other "meal" appearances. After Jesus has given his commission to the disciples he tells them "Lo, I am with you always, to the close of the age" (Matt. 28.20). Readers of Matthew's gospel would understand this promise of the real presence of Jesus to refer to his presence with them in the "breaking of bread." In that worship the disciples of all nations "see" Jesus.

In John's version of the Galilean appearance (John 21) we have all the elements that we find in other "meal" appearances. The setting is in the early morning, there is a lack of recognition, there is a sudden insight in the midst of a meal. This picture of all the world being drawn to Jesus comes as the result of the writer's skillful combination of two separate stories.

The appearances to the eleven that we are told about in the other gospels and in the Acts of the Apostles are not, as far as we can tell, set in Galilee. Yet they are all "meal" appearances. Pseudo-Mark tells us of an appearance to the two who "were walking into the country" (Mk. 16.12). This is probably a different version of the Emmaus account. Then he tells us of an appearance to the eleven "as they sat at table" (Mk. 16.14). Luke, in the most developed and longest of the resurrection stories, tells us of the appearance to the two disciples at Emmaus and "When he was at table with them, he took the bread and blessed and broke it and gave it to them and their eyes were opened and they recognized him" (Lk. 24.30, 31). These two then return to tell the eleven and "those who were with them" (Lk. 24.33) and Jesus appears at their meal and "ate before them" (Lk. 24.43). In John Chapter 20 we have two appearances to the disciples at the time of the evening meal. In Acts 1.4, as we have seen, the passage can read "appearing to them during forty days and speaking of the kingdom of God and while eating with them ..." (Acts 1.4b, 5a). Peter's sermon also includes the passage "not to all people, but to those who were chosen by God as witnesses, who ate and drank with him after he rose from the dead" (Acts 10.41).

The appearances to Peter and the twelve led directly to the establishment of the Church in Galilee. The "five hundred brethren" that Paul tells us about are those who came to share the experience of the disciples in Galilee. As they "broke bread" with the very people who had responded to the ministry of Jesus, there was Jesus in their midst. This had been the experience of the disciples, this came to be the experience of more than five hundred. The number may be meant to recall the feeding of the five thousand, perhaps at the very place. This "once for all" experience in Galilee had come to an end by the time Paul wrote his letter to Corinth.

Paul goes on to tell us that after these events, Jesus appeared to James and then to all the apostles and "last of all" to Paul himself. The parallelism is obvious, "once for all" to conclude the Galilean section, "last of all" to conclude the "Jerusalem" appearances.

We do not have a record of a separate appearance to James. It may be that again he was the first among the "brethren of the Lord" to recognize the presence of Jesus at a meal as Peter was first among the twelve. Certainly something happened that changed the attitude of a family that had opposed and rejected Jesus. Both Matthew and John tell us that the women at the tomb were directed to tell the "brethren" of the events. It is probable that many among the "brethren" came to be called "apostles." James the brother of the Lord is called an apostle by Paul in Gal. 1.19 in that wider sense in which Paul applied that term to himself, to Barnabas (1 Cor. 9.6) and to Andronicus and Junias (Rom. 16.7). The other brothers of Jesus (Matt. 13.55), Joseph, Simon and Judas and his sisters may also have belonged to that early band of evangelists. The names are the same as those of some of "the twelve" but there is no reason to suggest that these very common names refer to the same people.

Mary, the mother of Jesus and her family came up to Jerusalem for the paschal feast. Acts 1.14 tells us "all these with one accord devoted themselves to prayer, together with the women and Mary the mother of Jesus with his brothers." The leadership in Galilee may have soon returned to Jerusalem. John tells us that "Thomas, one of the twelve" (Jn. 20.24) returned to Jerusalem a week after the events at the tomb. The appearances recorded in John 20 to the disciples as they met at supper on Sundays and those recorded by Luke when Jesus appeared and ate with the eleven and "those who were with them" (Lk. 24.30, 33, Acts 1.4, 10.41) record what Paul summarizes as the appearances to "James, then to all the apostles" (1 Cor. 15.7).

The last appearance of the risen Lord was made to Paul. We were unable to accept the accounts of this event that we find in Acts. They contradict Paul's own accounts of his experience on many points. Paul was certain that his resurrection experience was similar to the others. He never cites it as an explanation of his own faith. It is cited only when he feels he must defend his position as an apostle, "Am I not an apostle? Have I not seen the Lord?" (1 Cor. 9.1). All we can say is that Paul felt that his experience was not a vision such as Luke has told us of but an actual appearance of Jesus. What form that appearance took we cannot tell but if almost every other appearance recorded took place in the context of a meal it would seem possible that Paul had a similar experience of the presence of Jesus at Damascus or Jerusalem.

The appearance of Jesus to Paul, "to one untimely born" or as we might put it "to one aborted," changed everything. All of Paul's theological understanding was influenced by this experience. While he spoke of how he preached "Christ crucified" (1 Cor. 1.23), in his ministry the resurrection was always part of his teaching. As Paul says in Romans 8.34 "It is Christ Jesus who died, yes (or perhaps "rather" or "more than that") who was raised from the dead." He tells the Corinthians that "If Christ has not been raised your faith is futile" (1 Cor. 15.17). Indeed the whole purpose of God's action in Christ is that he "died and lived again that he might be Lord of both the dead and the living" (Rom. 14.9).

We cannot begin to study the place of the resurrection in all of Paul's theology. His understanding of the Church as the risen body of Christ, of the sacraments as the instruments of the risen Christ, of faith, morality, suffering and death all studied in the light of the risen Christ, is all made possible in the outpouring of the Spirit by the glorified Christ. The resurrection was central in Paul's thoughts.

Jesus saw that his ministry and his preaching would probably bring him to a violent death. His adversaries had often tried to trap him. He knew what had happened to the prophets and to John the Baptist. He prepared his disciples for that fate. Yet, he looked to God to raise them so that they may drink wine "new" in the kingdom of God (Mk. 14.25, par.). If Jesus foresaw his death he also foresaw his resurrection, and if Matthew's version of this passage is authentic, he promised that he would drink together with his disciples in the end-time. We are told that Jesus looked forward to the day when "many will come from the East and West and sit at table with Abraham, Isaac and Jacob in the kingdom of heaven" (Matt. 8.11, par.).

The disciples therefore expected God to bring the end-time. When the eschatological age did not begin after Jesus was crucified, they were lost and uncertain. They had been told of the suffering that would come upon them. They had also been told that Jesus would be raised, judgement would begin and they would share in that judgement "sitting on twelve thrones." They had not been told, and perhaps Jesus did not realize, that they would find all that he had promised would be fulfilled within history rather than outside history. That new age, the age of the Spirit, would begin when the events that Jesus had promised would happen began to happen within history.

The disciples found Jesus present at their meals. They found that they were not taking part in that great messianic banquet of the end-time, it was just like old times. Jesus was present once again, just as he had been when they shared with him in his ministry of teaching and training. They experienced what the Church has come to call the "real presence." Just as the Church has never been able to come to agreement on what this expression means, so the gospel writers seem to find it difficult to explain how Jesus was seen to be present at these meals.

We have seen that the language used in the gospels of the appearances of Jesus is the ordinary language that would be used of ordinary perception. The words used are those that would be used to describe seeing a person in the natural world. Luke and John go out of their way to emphasize the physical nature of Jesus as he was present with his disciples. The language is the same as that used of his presence with them before the crucifixion.

Jesus, in these appearances, does move in a rather vaporous manner (Lk. 24.31, 36). He passes through walls (Jn. 20.19, 26). The disciples are often slow to recognize him (Matt. 28.17, Mk. 16.12, Lk. 24.30–32, 36–39, Jn. 20.15, 20, 25, 27, 21.4, 7, 12). Yet the point of these passages seems to be that Jesus appeared in a clear physical way and that seeing him was like seeing an ordinary object in the natural world. The reason for the hesitation of the disciples came from the unexpectedness of the appearance of Jesus.[178]

The gospel writers were certain that the appearances of Jesus were physical and real. The disciples believed that they had touched his body, that they had eaten a meal with him. They knew that they had watched him break bread and give it to them after the crucifixion just as he had broken bread with them so many times in those days before the crucifixion. In the past they had seen this as an acted parable of what was to come, the promise of a body broken. Now, after the resurrection, this act was a sign that the future kingdom they had worked toward with Jesus had been brought into the present. They were eating and drinking with Jesus, "new" in the kingdom of God.

The reestablishment of the special relationship that Jesus had built with his disciples began when they experienced his real presence in the breaking of bread. Almost every report that we have of the resurrection appearances of Jesus can be seen to support this understanding of the events. In this way the small group that had been broken and divided after their leader had been removed by crucifixion was brought together. When Jesus "took bread and broke it and gave it to them" they again began to find judgement, healing, forgiveness and freedom. The experience of the eleven came to others, to more than five hundred, to James and all the apostles and last of all to Paul. Through them that "faith is proclaimed in all the world" (Rom. 1.8). In the simple drama of a meal the disciples came to "rejoice in God through our Lord Jesus Christ" (Rom. 5.11).

Notes

1. The possibility of looking at the resurrection in this way is mentioned in Rowan Williams, *Resurrection*, Darton, Longman & Todd, London, 1982, pp. 39–40, 108–109, 115–16 and in Nicholas Lash, *Theology on the Way to Emmaus*, SCM Press, London, 1986, p. 81.
2. There are numerous surveys of these writings, the most comprehensive is in Peter Carnley, *The Structure of Resurrection Belief*, Clarendon Press, Oxford, 1987.
3. J.A.T. Robinson *Redating the New Testament*, SCM Press, London, 1976, suggests 30 for the Crucifixion, 33 for Paul's conversion, p. 37.
4. A.M. Ramsey, *The Resurrection of Christ*, Collins, London, 1945, p.9.
5. *Ibid.*, pp. 30–35.
6. *Ibid.*, p. 10.
7. *Ibid.*, p. 10.
8. Karl Barth, *Church Dogmatics*, T. & T. Clark, Edinburgh, 1958, p. 448.
9. R. Bultmann, *Primitive Christianity*, Meridian, Cleveland, 1956, p. 202.
10. R. Bultmann, *Kerygma and Myth*, S.P.C.K., London, 1953, p. 42.
11. R.H. Fuller, *The Formation of the Resurrection Narratives*, S.P.C.K., London, 1971, p.180.
12. *Ibid.*, p. 168.
13. *Ibid.*, p. 182.
14. E. Schillebeeckx, *Jesus*, Collins, London, 1979.
15. Both published by MacMillan, London.
16. M.J. Harris, *Raised Immortal*, Marshall, Morgan & Scott, London, 1983.
17. *Ibid.*, p.2.
18. *Ibid.*, p.7.
19. *Ibid.*, p. 12.
20. *Ibid.*, p. 43.
21. *Ibid.*, pp. 56 & 57.
22. *Ibid.*, pp. 69–71.
23. *Ibid.*, p. 6.
24. Norman Perrin, *The Resurrection According to Matthew, Mark and Luke*, Fortress Press, Philadelphia, 1977.
25. *Ibid.*, p. 3.
26. *Ibid.*, p. 33.
27. *Ibid.*, p. 30.
28. *Ibid.*, p. 34.

29. Norman Perrin, *Jesus and the Language of the Kingdom*, Fortress Press, Philadelphia, 1976, pp. 73–74.
30. Norman Perrin, *The Resurrection According to Matthew, Mark and Luke, op. cit.*, p. 37.
31. *Ibid.*, p. 38.
32. *Ibid.*, p. 46.
33. *Ibid.*, pp. 47–48.
34. *Ibid.*, p. 55.
35. *Ibid.*, p. 71.
36. *Ibid.*, p. 77.
37. Norman Perrin, *The New Testament, An Introduction*, Harcourt, Brace & Janosovitch, New York, 1974.
38. N. Perrin, *The Resurrection According to Matthew, Mark and Luke, op. cit.*, p. 80.
39. *Ibid.*, p. 82.
40. *Ibid.*, p. 83.
41. *Ibid.*, p. 83.
42. Willi Marxsen, *The Resurrection of Jesus of Nazareth*, Fortress Press, Philadelphia, 1970.
43. *Ibid.*, p. 76.
44. *Ibid.*, p. 77.
45. *Ibid.*, p. 78.
46. *Ibid.*, p. 93.
47. *Ibid.*, p. 92.
48. *Ibid.*, p. 125.
49. Willi Marxsen, *The Resurrection of Jesus as a Historical and Theological Problem*, published in English in *The Significance of the Message of the Resurrection for Faith in Jesus Christ*, Edited by C.F.D. Moule, SCM Press, London, 1968, pp.15–50.
50. Willi Marxsen, *The Resurrection of Jesus of Nazareth, op. cit.*, p. 78.
51. *Ibid.*, p. 126.
52. *Ibid.*, p. 126.
53. *Ibid.*, p. 147.
54. *Ibid.*, p. 77.
55. *Ibid.*, p. 125.
56. *Ibid.*, p. 128.
57. Peter Carnley, *The Structure of Resurrection Belief*, Clarendon Press, Oxford, 1987.
58. *Ibid.*, p. 18.
59. *Ibid.*, p. 225.
60. *Ibid.*, p. 242.
61. *Ibid.*, p. 248.
62. *Ibid.*, p. 295.
63. *Ibid.*, p. 296.
64. *Ibid.*, p. 314–5.
65. *Ibid.*, p. 324.
66. *Ibid.*, p. 366.

67. H. Riesenfeld, *The Gospel Tradition and its Beginnings; A study of the Limits of "Formgeschichte,"* Mowbray, London, 1957, and in *The Gospel Tradition,* Fortress Press, Philadelphia, 1970, pp. 1–29.
68. B. Gerhardsson, *The Origins of the Gospel Traditions,* Fortress Press, Philadelphia, 1979.
69. B. Reicke, *The Roots of the Synoptic Gospels,* Fortress Press, Philadelphia, 1986, pp. 180–181.
70. Werner Kelber, for example, has suggested that Mark wanted his written gospel to take priority over oral tradition; *The Oral and Written Gospel,* Fortress Press, Philadelphia, 1983, pp. 90–131.
71. C f., T. Bailey, "St. Mark VIII:27 again," *Studia Evangelica,* Vol. VII, Akademie-Verlag, Berlin, 1982.
72. Cf., E.P. Sanders, *Jesus and Judaism,* SCM Press, London, 1985, pp. 306–308.
73. *Ibid.,* p. 200–211.
74. C.R. Shepherd, *Small Groups,* Chandler Publishing Co., San Francisco, 1964, p. 1.
75. P. Vielhauer, *Gottesreich und Menschensohn in der Verkündigung Jesus Festschrift für Günther Dehn,* Kreis Moers, Neukirkchen, 1957, pp. 62–4.
76. E.P. Sanders, *Jesus and Judaism, op. cit.,* pp. 98–106.
77. *Sinaiticus, Vaticanus* and other texts add to the beginning of Mark Chapter 3 verse 16 "And he appointed the twelve." Appointed can be translated "created."
78. G. Strecker, *Der Weg der Gerechtigkeit: Untersuchung zur Theologie des Matthäus,* Vandenhoek & Ruprecht, Göttingen, 1962, pp. 95f.
79. F.H. Borsch, "Jesus, the Wandering Preacher?," in *What about the New Testament?,* Hooker & Hickling, eds., SCM Press, London, 1975, pp. 45–61.
80. Cf., E.P. Sanders, *Jesus and Judaism, op. cit.,* pp. 61–119.
81. A. Blumberg and R.T. Golembiewski, *Learning and Change,* Penguin Books, Harmondsworth, 1976, p. 13.
82. J.C. O'Neill, "Did Jesus teach that his death would be vicarious?," in *Suffering and Martyrdom in the New Testament,* W. Horbury & B.O. McNeil, Eds., C.U.P., Cambridge, 1981, pp. 9–27.
83. *Ibid.,* p. 12.
84. Vincent Taylor, *The Gospel according to St. Mark,* MacMillan & Co., London, 1955, p. 381.
85. Genesis Rabbah 56.3 (35c), Pesikta Rabbati 31.2 (143b), Tanhuma Wa'era 46, S. Buber Ed., (Wilna, 1885) Vol. 2, p. 114.
86. A. Meyer, *Jesu Muttersprache,* Freiburg 1 B & Leipzig, 1896, p. 78 also see Tertullian, Adv. Marc. III 18.2, Adv. Iud. 10.6.
87. J.C. O'Neill *op. cit.,* p. 15.
88. *Ibid.,* p. 17.
89. *Ibid.,* P. 17 & 18.
90. Philo, De Aq. 97, John 3.14f, Barnabas 12.7.
91. 2 Macc. 7.4, 4 Macc. 1.11, 6.27–29, 17.21f, Test. Ben.3.1, 6–8, Apoc. Elij. 3.33, Josephus, B.J. v. 9.4 (419).
92. J.C. O'Neill, *op. cit.,* p. 26.

93. Erich Dinkler attempts to answer the problems raised by these sayings by suggesting that Jesus required the disciples to be his "marked men." After the crucifixion the "mark" became the "cross." His suggestion is not convincing. (See Dinkler, "Jesu Wort vom Kreuztragen," In *Neutestamentliche Studien für Rudolf Bultmann zu seinem siebzigsten Gebürtstag*, 2nd edn., W. Eltester, ed., Töpelmann, Berlin, 1957, pp. 110–129).

94. F. Schussler-Fiorenza, *Foundational Theology*, Crossroads, N.Y., 1984, p. 21.

95. The literature is surveyed in John S. Pohee, *Persecution and Martyrdom in the Theology of Paul*, J.S.O.T. Press, Sheffield, 1985. Cf., J.P. Galvin, *Jesus' Approach to Death, an Examination of Recent Studies*, Theological Studies, Baltimore, MD, 41(4), 1980, pp. 713–744.

96. R. Bultmann, *Theology of the New Testament*, Vol. 1, SCM Press, London, 1952, p. 29.

97. Hans F. Bayer, *Jesus's Predictions of Vindication and Resurrection*, J.C.B. Mohr, Tübingen, 1986, p. 254.

98. Edward Lohse, *Märtyrer und Gottesknecht*, Vandenhoek & Ruprecht, Göttingen, 1955.

99. M.T. Kelsey, *Healing and Christianity*, Harper& Row, London, 1973, p. 57.

100. H.L. Strack and P. Billerbeck, *Kommentar zum Neuen Testament aus Talmud und Midrasch*, 5 vols., Beck, Munich, 1922–56, p. 480.

101. Cf., C.H. Dodd, *The Interpretation of the Fourth Gospel*, C.U.P., Cambridge, 1953, p. 372.

102. J.A.T. Robinson, *Twelve More New Testament Studies*, SCM Press, London, 1984, pp. 44–64.

103. R. Bultmann, *Theology of the New Testament*, Vol. 1, SCM Press, London, 1952, pp 23–24.

104. E.P. Sanders, *Paul and Palestinian Judaism*, SCM Press, London, 1977, p. 220.

105. *Ibid.*, p. 232.

106. The early Church soon felt a need for regular times of prayer and so we have the request in the Didache (8.3) "So you should pray three times a day."

107. J. Jeremias, *The Prayers of Jesus*, SCM Press, London, 1967, p. 73.

108. *Ibid.*, p. 76.

109. *Ibid.*, p. 97.

110. *Ibid.*, p. 63.

111. *Ibid.*, p. 43.

112. Tertullian, (De Pudicitia) 7–9.

113. R.C. Trench, *The Parables of our Lord*, London, MacMillan, 1841, p. 320.

114. A. Jülicher, *Die Gleichnisreden Jesu'*, J.C.B. Mohr, Tübingen, 1888, Vol. 2, 1899.

115. C.H. Dodd, *The Parables of the Kingdom*, Collins Fontana, London, 1963.

116. J. Jeremias, *The Parables of Jesus, op. cit.*, 1963.

117. *Ibid.*, p. 113.

118. *Ibid.*, pp. 115–230.

119. *Ibid.*, p. 214.

120. *Ibid.*, p. 215.

121. A. Jülicher, *op. cit.*, pp. 385–406.

122. J. Drury, *The Parables in the Gospels,* S.P.C.K., London, 1985, p. 67.
123. C.H. Dodd, *op. cit.,* p. 93.
124. *Ibid.,* pp. 97 & 98.
125. *Ibid.,* p. 92.
126. Karl Bornhäuser, *Die Bergpredigt,* Druck und Verlag von C. Bertelsmann, Gütersloh, 1923.
127. *Ibid.,* pp. 111,112.
128. *Ibid.,* pp. 8, 17.
129. Gerhard Lohfink argues that the "sermons" in Matthew and Luke were not addressed by Jesus to individuals or to humanity in general but to the twelve as representatives of Israel. Gerhard Lohfink, *Jesus and Community,* Fortress Press, Philadelphia, 1984, pp. 35–39.
130. Karl Bornhäuser, *op. cit.,* pp. 18–37.
131. *Ibid.,* pp. 70–78.
132. *Ibid.,* p. 92.
133. *Ibid.,* pp. 92 & 93.
134. *Ibid.,* p. 104.
135. *Ibid.,* pp. 145, 161.
136. W.O.E. Oesterley, *Sacrifices in Ancient Israel,* Hodder & Stoughton, London, 1937, p. 11f.
137. Johs Pedersen, *Israel,* Vol. III–IV, Oxford, O.U.P., 1946–47, p. 315f, cf., also F.N.C. Hicks, *The Fullness of Sacrifice,* 3rd edn., S.P.C.K., London, 1946, p. 11f.
138. G.A.F. Knight, *A Christian Theology of the Old Testament,* SCM Press, London, 1959, p. 284, cf., The Mishna, Tractate Yoma.
139. J.B. Josephus, *Antiquitates Judaicae,* Loeb Classical Library, XVLLL, London & Cambridge, MA, 1929–1943, pp. 116–19.
140. M. Goguel, *The Life of Jesus,* MacMillan, London, 1933, p. 266.
141. E.P. Sanders, *Jesus and Judaism, op.cit.,* 1985, p. 110.
142. *Ibid.,* p. 207.
143. *Ibid.,* p. 208.
144. R. Bultmann, *Theology of the New Testament, op. cit.,* p. 25.
145. E.P. Sanders, *Jesus and Judaism, op. cit.,* p. 117.
146. Norman Perrin, *Rediscovering the Teaching of Jesus,* Harper Row, New York, 1967, p. 102.
147. *Ibid.,* p. 104.
148. *Ibid.,* p. 106
149. E. Lohmeyer, *Lord of the Temple,* Oliver & Boyd, Edinburgh, 1961, pp.79f.
150. Norman Perrin, *Rediscovering the Teaching of Jesus, op. cit.,* p. 107.
151. *Ibid.,* p. 109.
152. *Ibid.,* p. 108.
153. J. Jeremias, *Eucharistic Words of Jesus,* Blackwell, Oxford, 1955, pp. 30f.
154. O. Cullmann, "The Meaning of the Lord's Supper in Primitive Christianity," in *Essays on the Lord's Supper,* O. Cullman and F.J. Leenhardt Eds., E.T. Lutterworth Press, London, 1958.

155. Tertullian, *De Corona Militis 3* (Pl 2:99), Hyppolytus, *Apostolic Tradition 21* (Botte LQF 56,57) also *The New Catholic Encyclopedia*.
156. See cover photo of Byzantine mosaic at the Church of the Multiplication, Tabgha, Lake Galilee.
157. N. Hass, *Anthropological Observations on the Skeletal Remains from Giv'at Ha-Mivtar*, Israel Exploration Journal 20, 1970, pp. 38–59.
158. J.C. O'Neill, *Messiah*, Cochrane Press, Cambridge, 1980, p. 75.
159. J. Jeremias, *The Eucharistic Words of Jesus, op. cit.*, pp. 103–107.
160. E.L. Bode, *The First Easter Morning*, Biblical Institute Press, Rome, 1970, p. 144f. After thorough study of all the texts involved, Bode concludes that Christian Sunday worship began with the visit to the tomb that morning. He tells us that this answer to the question about the beginning of Sunday worship is superior to any other answer that has been proposed.
161. B. Lindars, *New Testament Apologetic*, SCM Press, London, 1961, p. 59f.
162. R.H. Fuller, *op. cit.*, pp. 23–27.
163. A.D. Churchill, *The Resurrection of Christ*, unpublished D. Phil. thesis, Oxford, 1968.
164. R.M. Machowski, *Jerusalem—City of Jesus*, Eerdmans, Grand Rapids, 1980, p. 158f. Also Mo'ed Katan 27b.
165. R. Bultmann, *The History of the Synoptic Tradition*, Blackwell, Oxford, 1963, p. 287–290.
166. H. Grass, *Ostergeschehen und Osterberichte*, 2nd edn., Vandenhoeck und Ruprecht, Göttingen, 1962, p. 183–184.
167. R.E. Brown, *The Birth of the Messiah*, Doubleday, New York, 1977, pp 111–116.
168. T.L. Donaldson, *Jesus on the Mountain*, J.S.O.T. Press, Sheffield, 1985, p. 253 n33.
169. K. Barth, *The Resurrection of the Dead*, English Trans. H.J. Stenning, Hodder and Stoughton, London, 1933, pp. 119–120.
170. R.H. Fuller, *op. cit.*, p. 91.
171. *Ibid.*, p. 154.
172. Refers, after Jewish usage, to the following Sunday, not the Monday. N.E.B. rightly has 'a week later.''
173. O. Linton, *The Third Aspect: A Neglected Point of View: A Study in Gal. i–ii and Acts ix and xv*, Studia Theologica 3, 1949, pp. 79–95.
174. J. Knox, *Chapters in the Life of Paul*, Abingdon-Cokesbury, New York, 1950, pp. 13–89.
175. R.H. Fuller, *op. cit.* p. 106–107.
176. O. Cullman, *Early Christian Worship*. SCM Press, London, 1953, p. 15f.
177. G.C. Homans, *The Human Group*, Routledge, Kegan Paul, London, 1951, p. 170.
178. See the summary in C.F. Evans, *Resurrection and the New Testament*, SCM Press, London, 1970, p. 59–61.

Author Index

There is little in recent books on the resurrection of Christ, William Lunny argues, that is of help to the ordinary pastor. Their technicalities obscure the central element of the Christian faith. However, the evidence has to be examined and evaluated.

The most successful way to do this, William Lunny has found, is to see the resurrection of Jesus in terms of the re-formation of a small group. During his ministry Jesus grouped disciples around him and trained them for their role in his mission; here the meals they shared were very special. That life together was shattered by the crucifixion, but the group again found Jesus with them in the 'breaking of bread'.

In presenting this approach in detail, the book begins with a survey of the reports of the resurrection. It then looks at some recent resurrection studies by leading New Testament scholars. The third part investigates the nature of the training of the Twelve, and the last part 'Eating with the Lord', assesses the resurrection appearances.

William Lunny has been parish priest at St Dunstan's, Victoria, British Columbia for the past eighteen years.

Cover: Byzantine mosaic from the Church of the Multiplication at Tabgha on Lake Galilee (photo: W.J. Lunny)

ISBN 0-334-02335-1

£6.95 net

9 780334 023357